The Power of Music: Mobilisation among Islamic Movements

Joseph Alagha

KNOWLEDGE WORLD
KW Publishers Pvt Ltd
New Delhi

in association with

Calcutta University
Kolkata

2011 FPBA BEST PUBLISHERS AWARD (ENGLISH)

The Court of Directors of the East India Company sent a despatch in July, 1854 to the Governor-General of India in Council, suggesting the establishment of the Universities of Calcutta, Madras and Bombay.

In pursuance of that despatch, the University of Calcutta was founded on January 24, 1857.

The University adopted in the first instance, the pattern of the University of London and gradually introduced modifications in its constitution.

ISBN 978-93-81904-34-3

KNOWLEDGE WORLD

Published in India by

Kalpana Shukla
KW Publishers Pvt Ltd
4676/21, First Floor, Ansari Road, Daryaganj, New Delhi 110002
Phone: +91.11.23263498/43528107
email: knowledgeworld@vsnl.net • www.kwpub.com

Printed and Bound in India

"An Outstanding Academic Contribution." Prof. **Laudan Nooshin**, Senior Lecturer in Ethnomusicology, City University, London.

Praise for earlier work on cultural politics:

"Pious Entertainment: Hizbullah's Islamic Cultural Sphere", in: *Muslim Rap, Halal Soaps and Revolutionary Theater: Artistic Developments in the Muslim World*, edited by Karin van Nieuwkerk. (Austin: University of Texas Press, 2011), pp. 149-175.

Alagha's chapter on Hezbollah's Islamic cultural sphere is sure to generate some of the most interesting discussions. Lebanon, and Hezbollah in particular, are among the hottest topics in the studies of contemporary Islam. Few people actually have the appropriate levels of both—access to and understanding of Hezbollah areas and personalities to do an adequate job of analysing the ever growing body of cultural production the movement generates. Equally important is the demonstrable ease with which he can enter into the theological debates surrounding the lawfulness of music, bringing the expertise of an Islamologist to a discussion often dominated by scholars of cultural studies who don't have such a depth of knowledge. His discussion of the transition from *al-hala al-Islamiyya* [Islamic religio-political sphere] to *al-saha al-Islamiyya* [Islamic cultural sphere] is extremely important and exciting, particularly since his sources include the highest echelons of Hezbollah's leadership. Finally, his discussion of how leading Shi'i thinkers have declared that cultural production has to be central to the construction of revolution has far-reaching implications that most scholars in the field have yet to consider. If Alagha's chapter shows how Shi'i thinking is at the forefront of the changing Islamic attitude towards music, it points to the very different ways that Hezbollah conceives of both culture and the role of religion in public life.

Anonymous reviewer of the **University of Texas Press**

Joseph Alagha's 'Pious Entertainment: Hizbullah's Islamic Cultural Sphere' offers a useful counterpoint to Frishkopf's analysis as he focuses not on diaspora aesthetic production but on how one movement work to transform all art in 'the art of resistance', into an art form that resists not mere tyranny and oppression but 'purposeless art', or 'art for the sake of art' at the same time. Alagha explores the transformation between religious-political and specific cultural spheres in the Shi'a Islam of Lebanon. While Hezbollah's well-known record of violence leads many to assume the group's governing ideology to be quite constraining when it comes to culture, the movement actively demarcates between orthodoxy at the ritual or theological level, and a 'pluralistic Islamic cultural sphere where the concept of citizenship reigns; where all people have equal rights and duties, and where coexistence and mutual respect are the main norm' (151). This view is articulated within a larger need to sponsor 'purposeful art' that allows Muslims to remain close to God, and politically mobilised during their leisure time as well as at work.

Mark LeVine is a professor of History at the University of California, Irvine, and a distinguished visiting professor at the Centre for Middle Eastern Studies, Lund University, Sweden.

Contents

To my teacher and inspirer,
Prof. Arda A. Ekmekji, with
love, respect, and appreciation

The Power of Music: Mobilisation among Islamic Movements

Abstract

This article discusses the cultural politics of the Taliban and Hizbullah. While Hizbullah embraces 'resistance art' and encourages purposeful music and artistic expressions, the Taliban censure music and restrict artistic activities, considering them innovations (*bida'*), which distract from practicing 'authentic Islam' and 'true worship'. To discuss the interplay between 'power of music' and 'music in power', this study uses samples of *anashid* (songs, hymns, and anthems) of the Taliban and Hizbullah who practice music with a jihadist stance as an empowering mechanism. Unlike Hizbullah, the Taliban's views on music boil down to edicts and prohibitions, censuring music, musicians, and musical instruments. Whilst Hizbullah sanctions within certain religious safeguards—'fun' or pious entertainment as a required human necessity—the Taliban consider these as evils that lead to man's degeneration and the destruction of his moral fibre, thus, downgrading his aspiration to come closer to God.

Keywords:

Resistance art, resisting public, cultural production, music-power nexus, resource mobilisation

This article is divided into two parts: a thesis and an antithesis. In the thesis, engineer Khalid Baig, a seemingly intellectual defender of the Taliban, argues against four notions: (1) *jihad* with music, by contending that singing cannot be an act of worship of Allah; (2) purposeful art (*al-fann al-hadif*), by regarding it as a mass delusion; (3) pious entertainment, by considering it as totally un-Islamic; and (4) the use of music in supplication and Islamic propagation (*da'wa*), by deeming it conducive to self-gratification, rather than serving Allah (Baig 2008). In other words, Baig represents the genre of ideologically motivated literature on the subject. Baig promotes what looks on surface value as a 'scholarly' argument in order to realise his project of demonstrating that music and musical instruments are banned in the absolute.

In the antithesis, I have argued that a scholarly approach is possible; indeed, several scholars or movements now stipulate conditions under which music is allowed, and argue for art with a mission, or allow the permissibility of music for Islamic propagation (Cf. Van Nieuwkerk 2011); Khalid Baig denies all these possibilities. In the age of fragmentation of religious authority, Baig claims that his book is a strong scholarly work, that all the important sources have been used, and that this is the final academic viewpoint.[1] Baig ends his book by calling on all people to destroy their musical instruments.[2] Since the Taliban regard music as an 'abomination of the Devil' (5:90), in line with them, Baig only sanctions listening to 'cassette tape[s] of speech'.[3] The book sometimes reads more like a defence and justification of the Taliban's actions, rather than a scholarly analysis of music. Baig's book appears to be convincing since scholars without a firm background in Islamic studies could potentially read it as a scholarly work. Influenced by his approach, some authors and Muslim Internet forums[4] have already uncritically referred to his book thinking it is foundational, generalising that this is the view of normative Islam as Baig would like them to believe. For that reason, it is important to take his work seriously, and to deconstruct his reading of sources that omit all kinds of liberal or contextual readings. Most likely, Baig's work stands in sharp contrast to the progressive ways several religious scholars, Islamist movements, and post-Islamist organisations have been taking to (re)interpret sources, and to show the many contexts in which music and listening to music is allowed.

Thesis

Introduction

As a promotional book review, in the 'Forward', Syed Salman Nadvi boasts Baig's credentials: an 'academically sound book' written by an engineer who has a 'remarkable proficiency in Islamic scholarship... The author's own academically superb and scholarly introduction'[5]... 'quite a good discussion' by 'comprehensively referring not only to original sources but also to contemporary works in Arabic, Urdu, and English'... 'indicate the author's grasp of the subject'.[6] Baig continues his propaganda in the 'preface' by portraying the saliency of his book, which he compiled, with two other books over a period of five years, with the help of his two daughters and son, making the end product appear as a family endeavour, in a book that aims at 'getting clarity on the issue of music'.[7] Baig adds, "This book is an attempt to reduce this cacophony by taking a deep look at Islam's stance on music and singing from historic, cultural, and jurisprudential perspectives."[8] In the 'Introduction', Baig clarifies more the goal of his book: "The purpose of the book is then... to expose those extraneous forces and make the historical discussion on music among scholars accessible to the readers so we can cut that controversy to size. I aim at explaining the answers already given by well-known authorities so we can easily evaluate the new answers being promoted today from some quarters both within the Muslim world and without."[9] On scrutiny, it turns out that, in many instances, Baig refers to obscure authorities or fails to name his so-called 'well-known authorities'.

A Synopsis of Baig's Argument

Khalid Baig's book is composed of twelve chapters, arranged thematically into three parts, four appendixes, a bibliography, and an index. Part one, which is divided into four chapters, offers the theoretical and historical background. Chapter one, entitled 'Islam and Poetry', stresses the importance of the oral tradition in Arab-Islamic cultural heritage. Chapter two deals with 'Music Before and After Islam' by surveying the history of music, and societal attitudes towards it from the pre-Islamic pagan period of ignorance (*Jahiliyya*) to the 19th century. Chapter three, entitled 'Music and the Media Revolution', elaborates on the technological inventions of the gramophone, the radio transistor, the film industry and television, and their impact on musical cultural productions. Baig breaks the flow of the argument with his 'Perspective on Technology'. He vehemently criticises westernisation, globalisation, and technology—equating westernisation with globalisation.[10]

In chapter four, Baig reveals his loathe for orientalists, painting a grim picture of their scholarship. In particular, he takes issue with 'ethnomusicologists or the subgroup of orientalists with a special interest in the music in the Muslim world'.[11] He contends that their 'works feed each other, each author perpetuating the fabrications ('misunderstandings') of his predecessor while adding his own creativity [...]. orientalists [...] openly declared their enmity to Islam [...] The act maybe an outgrowth of their frustration over Islam's great success in keeping its acts of worship music-free'.[12] Baig censures the well-renowned George Farmer: "But what he lacks in arguments or evidence, he tries to make up for with a fertile imagination and a venomous pen. Of these he has no shortage."[13] He accuses Farmer of fabricating 'juicy tales' while employing 'the flimsiest evidence he can get his hands on."[14]

The second part, entitled 'Clearing the Fog', forms the core of the book. It endeavours to survey the polemics pertaining to music production, transition, and consumption, from the advent of Islam until current times, cautioning that 'today the economic motive behind indulgence in music is stronger than ever'.[15] Baig follows debates informed by the scholarly tradition about the lawfulness and the unlawfulness of music and its categorisation scaling from the permitted (*halal*), the reprehensible (*makruh*), to the forbidden (*haram*). In chapters five and six, he confines himself to the two primary sources of Islamic law (*Shari'a*) —the Qur'an and *hadith*—selectively discussing the verses and *ahadith*, which sanction music and prohibit it.

Along the same lines, chapter seven discusses 'The Views of Early Muslims', that is, 'the Companions, Successors, and early Muslim authorities'[16] who considered music as either reprehensible or prohibited[17] and noted their 'abhorrence of musical instruments'.[18] In chapter eight, entitled 'Sama' [spiritual songs]: The Sufi Perspective' and chapter nine, entitled 'The Case for Malahi [musical instruments]', Baig takes great care in refuting arguments in support of listening to music and musical instruments. He censures Shaykh 'Abd al-Ghani al-Nabulsi for arguing that there is nothing intrinsically wrong with music in itself.[19] Interestingly, Baig extends his criticism to Imam al-Ghazali, but first he extols him as 'a great scholar who dealt a serious blow to deviant sects', contending that the *umma* 'remains indebted to him'. Then

Baig shifts ground: 'But ultimately, he [al-Ghazali] was a human being; genius but not infallible [...] other scholars embraced Ihya' [his book] but took exception to his argument for sama'. Ultimately, the Ummah is greater than its greater scholars are'.[20]

In chapter ten, entitled 'The Ruling of the Jurists', Baig asserts without any qualification the fulcrum of his entire book: "The fact [is] that there are broad areas of agreement between all schools of Islamic law [madhahib] regarding today's music [...] most music filling the airwaves in the Muslim world today does so over vehement Hanafi, Maliki, Shafi'i, Sufi, and Shi'ah objections."[21]

The third part of the book 'Where Now?' is supposed to present his most important findings. In chapter eleven, entitled 'Music in Muslim Society Today', and in the concluding chapter twelve, entitled 'Beyond the Debate', Baig assertively repeats his unsubstantiated claim, namely, that since 'the great majority of scholars declare prohibition', when 'we sincerely pay heed to such advice, [then] the music issue may become easy to sort out'.[22] Bearing in mind his repeated dictum that 'we have been conditioned to consider music as normal and acceptable, indeed absolutely unavoidable'[23] and 'No doubt, music is an essential component in the 'approved' Islam and promotion of music is an important strategic goal',[24] Baig admonishes the youth not to follow the piped piper. He urges them instead to take 'a U-turn on the issue of music' as a precursor to 'a turn around in a person's life' by banning music in the absolute and destroying all musical instruments.[25]

Antithesis

"Without music no state could survive."

— Molière

Overall, Baig's book has several shortcomings: (1) it is marred with subjectivity, contradictions, digressions, and lack of the contextual approach; (2) the claim that there is no music in the mosque and in Islam's acts of worship is superficial and superfluous; and (3) the contention that there are no differences among schools and opinions of scholars is unwarranted.

Concerning the lack of the contextual approach, throughout his book, he curtly discusses or simply dismisses any argument for sanctioning music. Baig does not give due attention to the religious sensibilities of the audience pertaining to religious prohibitions (*al-mahazir al-shar'iyya*) and religious safeguards (*al-dawabit al-shar'iyya*), ignoring to mention the context, circumstances, and setting. In other words—in his non-contextual arguments—Baig does not discuss the limitations imposed on music, and which test cases stretch these limits. In both Sunni and Shi'ite jurisprudence, human and social contexts dictate a flexible approach to adjudication in Islamic law. According to Shaykh Yusuf al-Qaradawi,[26] Tariq Ramadan, Ayatullah Sayyid Muhammad Husayn Fadlallah, and Muhammad Jawad Mughniyyé, just to name a few, the contextual approach is important to a proper understanding and interpretation of the *Shari'a*. The principles of jurisprudence (*usual al-fiqh*), the maxims of Islamic jurisprudence (*qawa'id al-fiqh*), and especially the purposes of the *Shari'a* (*maqasid al-Shari'a*) convey that the *Shari'a* was revealed to the human beings because of interest (*maslaha*) for reinterpretation of the law, all give precedence to the contextual approach. Since Islam is social practice, there is no *Shari'a* in the absolute. *Shari'a* as a socially constructed phenomenon, does not fall short of guiding a modern life, does have the flexibility and pragmatism to deal with man's progress, and addresses both the generalities and particularities that have to do with man's necessities and needs (Ramadan 2009: 101-112; Mughniyyé 1988: 225-232, 363-365). Since his book is ideological, rather than academic, Baig bypasses the contextual argument, thus reducing the complexity, flexibility, and pragmatism of Muslim jurisprudence to individual whim, quoting out of context in order to prove that 'music and singing is prohibited' (Baig 2008: 252).

Concerning the second shortcoming, Baig dogmatically asserts, "There is no controversy regarding the use of music in the *masjid* [mosque], which has remained a music-free zone for more than fourteen centuries" (Baig 2008: 97). It seems Baig forgot that the Prophet allowed the Ethiopians to dance with their spears in his mosque (Qaradawi 2004: 7); he set a precedent by singing in a mosque; and that the rightly guided caliph and companion 'Umar sanctioned the singing of a Shaykh after he performed the duty of prayer ('Amara 1999: 11-13).

Most likely, Baig seems quite unaware that—in line with Imam Khumayni who stressed that a *nashid* could become an obligatory duty in some battles—Hizbullah broadcasted its revolutionary *anashids*, via loud speakers, from the mosques' minarets in celebration of every military victory the Party accomplished against its enemies. Furthermore, Baig seems non-conversant that Imam 'Ali Khamina'i, the current spiritual leader of Iran, sanctioned chanting religious or revolutionary anashid with musical instruments at the mosque in between two prayers or after the evening prayers, especially if they are used for mobilisation purposes, as long as this activity does not conflict with the duty of prayer (Khamina'i 2009: 171-172).

Trotting the religious sensibilities of Christians, Baig addresses the Christian doctrine. He writes, "We need to contrast Islam's record with that of Christianity, because Islam succeeded precisely where Christianity failed [...] Islam banished music from its acts of worship" (Baig 2008: 96). Baig presents counter-evidence when he concedes that the so-called 'misguided Sufis' or 'errant Sufis' used 'music during hajj' and '*sama'* with duffs and flutes' during supplication (*du'a'*) (Baig 2008: 96). It seems that the Sufis and other heterodox groups are not considered Muslims by him.

Regarding the third shortcoming, Baig's one-sided analysis is clearly portrayed in chapter ten in which he claims that all schools of law (*Madhahib*) ban music. I beg to differ with his doctrinaire views. The canonical book entitled *Al-Fiqh 'ala Al-Madhahib Al-Arba'a* unequivocally demonstrates that the four Sunni schools of law sanction music within certain contexts, and that there is no prohibition in the absolute on listening to music and playing certain musical instruments that were sanctioned by the Prophetic tradition. (See for instance, volume II, *Hukum Al-Ghina'* [The Ruling on Music], pp. 36-39).

Further, Baig's book is far from being representative of the Shi'ite and Salafi positions. Baig's misleading approach and way of argumentation that brushes aside leading *'ulama'* seems untenable on many grounds. He chooses Hammud—an obscure, unrepresentative Shi'ite figure who is not even a Shi'ite religious authority (*marja'*)—as the representative of the

Shi'ite views on music and generalises his findings to include all music, when Hammud confines them only to music in weddings, as the title and contents of his book convey (2005: 246-250). Even then, Baig quotes Hammud selectively, that is, only those parts that substantiate his argument, leaving out those that refute it. Most importantly, Hammud clearly sanctions all the wailing rituals (*marathi*) associated with the *'Ashura'* ritual commemorating the death of Imam Husayn in *Karbala'*, in Iraq centuries ago in 61 AH/680 AD (Hammud 2005: 149-185). Hammud unequivocally states: "Singing is prohibited when it leads to *tarab* [enchantment],[27] and in the *marathi* there is no *tarab*" (Hammud 2005: 175), that is, the *marathi* is permissible. This is the standard view of leading *marja*'s such as Ayatullahs Fadlallah (August 04, 2009 interview) and al-Khu'i (al-Khu'i 1990: 702); Sistani;[28] Khumayni (Al-Hamidi 1994: 114); and Khamina'i (2009: 166). Maybe the reason behind Baig ignoring a quarter of Hammud's book on the wailing rituals is that the Taliban prohibited the Shi'ites from commemorating Imam Husayn's *marathi* during the month of *muharram* of every year (Sarafraz 2008: 140).

In less than two pages, Baig presents the Salafi position, basing his argument on a selective reading of one book of the late Shaykh Muhammad Nasir al-Albani (1914-99) (Baig 2008: 245-246). However, Baig does not mention al-Albani's salient *fatwa* on *anashid* (songs, hymns, and anthems), namely, 'If the *anashid* have Islamic connotations, and were not accompanied by musical instruments, then they are welcome. However, two stipulations have to be met: (1) The *anashid* have to be free of any *shar'i* violations such as *laghu*[29] (foolish talk) and the like, and (2) not to become a habit or custom (*daydan*) that distracts its listeners from (a) reading the Qur'an, which is a Sunna injunction, (b) keep the listeners away from aspiring to beneficial knowledge, and (c) Islamic propagation (*al-da'wa*) to God Almighty.[30] Although Baig chose to refer only to one current of Salafism—the purist, apolitical form of al-Albani to the exclusion of others—it seems that was counterproductive, since even al-Albani does not ban music in the absolute.

In short, it seems Baig did not exercise due diligence with his text causing the imperatives of his ideological background to trump those of scholarship. Despite its initial academic appearance, the book contains numerous errors and contradictions, ranging from very basic factual errors, to errors in scholarly judgments, to errors of attribution. Thus, it ought to be shunned in all respects since it hampers the many interesting developments and discussions going on within the Muslim world with regard to music and Islam.

How does Creativity in Art Comport with Pain and Suffering?

It seems creativity in art is always accompanied by pain and suffering, as Lebanese composers and musicians stress. The late Tawfiq Al-Basha, author of the five-part 'Beirut Symphony 1982', protesting the Israeli invasion of Lebanon, argued that music is his prayer and temple after God. Abd Al-Rahman Al-Basha, Tawfiq's son, stressed that there is no civilization without music; that the source of music is divine. Highlighting the role of cultural mobilisation, Ahmad Qa'bur, author of 'I Call upon You' (*Unadikum*)[31] —the most listened to revolutionary song embodying the suffering of the Palestinian people—suggested that life without music is miserable. Since its release in 1975, it became the emblem of the Palestinian resistance. Stressing the idea that music is often used to represent struggle, renowned Lebanese composer Elias al-Rahbanni asserted that cultural, intellectual, and artistic expressions of resistance are historically rooted and are, in that sense, perennial. For him, art signifies resistance, struggle, challenge, and a perpetual revolution (Crete 2008; 97, 34, 40, 120, 70). Why is art accorded such an important mobilisation role?

Historically, the link between 'music production, dissemination, representation, and reception' (Nooshin 2009: 1) on the one hand, and power or the exercise of political power on the other, is not new. It is confined neither to Islamic movements nor to secular ones, but has been in the works for centuries. In studying the music-power nexus, Nooshin questions, "What is it about music that enables it to permeate every area of human life, weaving together political and aesthetic in ways which are at times overt, at others so subtle that nothing can match its power" (2009: 2, 31). As such, music becomes a means of self-empowerment aimed at exercising social and political control, or people employ it as an act of defiance (Nooshin 2009: 159, 163, 31).

Nooshin's argument can be well illustrated by the two cases of the Lebanese Shi'ite resistance movement Hizbullah on the one hand, and the Afghani Taliban on the other, who have both earned a reputation for militancy and violence. It is interesting to compare the two because Hizbullah changed its ideological positions by embracing cultural production, predominantly through music and artistic expressions, while the Taliban censored music and restricted cultural activities.

In this article, I aim to address certain questions: (1) In which way Hizbullah and the Taliban can be viewed as 'resistance publics'—as a counter cultural identity against the hegemonic power and lack of its legitimacy? In other words, how does music become a space for challenging and/or resisting certain dominant ideologies or holders of power? (Nooshin 2009: 3). (2) How can the *anashid* and the *tarana*s positively contribute to the war effort of Hizbullah and the Taliban respectively? In other words, how does music accumulate symbolic power/capital in special and exclusive ways? (Nooshin 2009: 3). (3) How can music be exploited as a mobilisation medium that is conducive to *jihad* (struggle in the way of God) and militancy against Hizbullah's and the Taliban's enemies? Are Hizbullah's *anashid* and the Taliban's *tarana*s such types of 'music'? As Nooshin (2009: 3) puts it, how does music develop into a medium of agency and empowerment, and which types of music can act as an intermediary in the process of power struggle, negotiation, and bargaining?

In order to answer these questions, I divide this article into five main sections. Section one offers a theoretical perspective from the stance of power and cultural production. Section two gives samples of the Taliban's *tarana*s and Hizbullah's *anashid*, arguing that both—as 'resisting publics'—practice some kind of jihad with music as an empowerment mechanism, although the means differ.[32] In this process, the Taliban and Hizbullah accumulate symbolic capital. Sections three and four discuss the Taliban's and Hizbullah's views on music, or the different ways they legitimise or rationalise the role of 'music' in the process of power struggle, negotiation, and bargaining. Section five compares the views of Hizbullah and the Taliban on music in terms of actual practice. In other words, this section endeavours to answer the question of how do their views on music comport with reality. Noteworthy, the ideological differences between the Taliban and Hizbullah cannot be generalised as differences between the Sunnis and Shi'ites as such.

Concerning sources, I gathered information on the Taliban predominantly from open accesses English and Arabic secondary sources,[33] while I compiled most of the information on Hizbullah from field research, interviews, and primary Arabic sources. In order to discuss themes such as the legitimacy of music in Islam, the feasibility of constructing a music theory, and Islamic movements that function as resisting publics, I embarked on fieldwork visits to Lebanon. In addition to primary Arabic internet sources and secondary sources in Arabic and English, I was able to obtain a host of primary Arabic sources; I conducted interviews in Hizbullah's bastion in southern Beirut (*al-Dahiya*) with Shi'ite religious authorities and Hizbullah's authoritative cadres on the issue of jihad with music in relation to the three themes above. For this, I interviewed the three heads of Hizbullah's cultural politics organizations—Shaykh Shafiq Jaradi, the Rector of *Al-Ma'arif Al-Hikmiyya* College, Skaykh 'Ali Daher and Muhammad Kawtharani, the head and deputy of Hizbullah's Cultural Unit, and Shaykh Akram Barakat, the head of the *Cultural Islamic Al-Ma'arif Association* as well as other important cadres who weigh in on such debates. Other notable Hizbullah figures I have interviewed are Hajj Muhammad Ra'd, *Shura* (Consultative) Council member and the head of Hizbullah's parliamentary bloc; MP 'Ali Fayyad, professor of political sociology at the Lebanese University, the head of Hizbullah's educational mobilisation unit, and the former director of the Party's think tank the Consultative Center of Studies and Documentation (CCSD); Hajj Ghalib Abu Zaynab, party officer for Muslim-Christian dialogue; MP Nawwaf al-Musawi, the Party's philosopher *par excellence* and ex-foreign relations officer, and Sayyid Ibrahim al-Musawi, Hizbullah's spokesman.

It is interesting to compare heuristically the Taliban and Hizbullah, since as divergent their views on music and cultural productions seem to be, both legitimise their views by reference to Islamic sources. Most notably their adoption of the concept of *'amal al-ihsan* (action of excellence under God's guidance), and texts which promote them as Islamic, is established in Shi'ite thinking and traditions, as well as Sunni traditions. This common ground of thinking between Hizbullah and the Taliban is warranted in Qur'anic verses such as (3:26), which stress that 'all good is from Allah', in order to validate the idea of an Islamic state that develops by acceptance of good, rather than by any form of stereotypical imposition. Thus, there is a rational theological basis for believing that all good is from God, that good will ultimately shape government, and that the resultant society is inherently Islamic (Sarafraz 2008: 114-122; Jaradi October 21, 2009 interview). Interestingly, although both the Taliban and Hizbullah dwell on the same Qur'anic concept, Hizbullah uses it to sanction music and cultural productions, while the Taliban employ it to ban both. What they have in common is that as resisting publics, both Hizbullah and the Taliban seem to regard revolutionary *anashid* as a form of self-disciplined mobilisation and empowerment aimed at contesting the social and political control of the hegemonic power—the Lebanese state in Hizbullah's case, and foreign invades in the Taliban case. While Hizbullah played its revolutionary *anasid* from mosque minarets, it seems that the Taliban banned various genres of music in order to promote their *taranas* (*anashid*, chants) as the only acceptable Islamic form of chanting.

Baily observed that the more censorship and restrictions are imposed on music, the more that Islamic society is conservative and traditional; and the more music thrives in a tolerant atmosphere, the more progressive that Islamic society is since 'music is a sensitive indicator of a whole set of other values and attitudes'. In other words, Baily argues that the conditions and restrictions that are imposed on music are, in some way, an indication of various levels of Islamic orthodoxy (Baily 2009: 143-163). It will be demonstrated that as 'resisting publics', the Taliban more likely fit Baily's first characterisation, while Hizbullah most probably manifests the second. Hizbullah labels purposeful art, 'art with a mission' (*al-fann al-hadif*), or, more precisely, 'resistance art', as ideologically motivated art, which aims at rectifying individuals and reforming society by portraying art as pious-moral productions that are in line with Islamic values and norms.

Power and Cultural Production: The Case of Music

In this section, the concepts of 'resistance identity' and 'project identity' will be made relevant for the analysis of the Taliban's and Hizbullah's cultural production, especially music and chanting.

In studying what makes music so powerful, and 'how that power might be harnessed for performances of reconciliation instead of conflict', Nooshin argues that since music 'lends itself to the expression, negotiation and circulation of power', then 'power is thoroughly implicated in the social practices of music', and 'music is so thoroughly implicated in the exercise of power' (2009: 25, 2, 16). Therefore, it is plausible to look into the concept of power as such, and how it comports with the notion of resistance to established authority.

Identity Construction: From 'Resistance Identity' to 'Project Identity'

I am not going to discuss identity constructions on an individual level; rather, I will look at identity processes of socio-political movements for which the concept of resource mobilisation plays a crucial role.

Resource mobilisation refers to the way a social movement mobilises its resources and/or capitals (religious, political, symbolic, and socio-economic) in order to confront and survive strategic difficulties and challenges facing it. Thus, a social movement constructs its identity in order to adjust to a world that is in incessant flux, or else it will risk demise or might not remain a dynamic social movement. Castells defines a social movement as 'purposive collective actions whose outcome, in victory as in defeat, transforms the values and institutions of society' (1998: 3). Fuller notes that Islamism 'represents the single most important [mobilisation] force for political change across the Muslim world' (2003: 24). He adds, "Islamists are good at identifying and articulating the grievances, but to succeed they must move beyond their present roles if they wish to remain relevant to societies' needs. This is an example of where resource mobilisation could be useful. Thus, Islamism is 'a religious-cultural-political framework for engagement on issues that most concern politically engaged Muslims" (2003: 193). It seems this religious-cultural-political framework constitutes the foundation of Hizbullah's cultural politics.

In Castells' theory of identity, the concepts of 'resistance identity' and 'project identity' play a salient role in exemplifying resistance and defiance to established authority. As a working definition of identity, I employ Castells' definition of resistance identity since it deals with the question of oppression and resistance, which influence the identity of a social movement (1998: 9). According to Castells, conceptually, resistance identity is 'generated by those actors that are in positions/conditions devaluated and/or stigmatised by the logic of domination, thus building trenches of resistance and survival on the basis of principles different from, or opposed to, those permeating the institutions of society' (1998: 8; Cf. Calhoun 1994:17). He adds that empirically speaking, resistance identities are not confined to traditional values since they could be moulded by progressive social movements. These social movements opt for the alternative to set up an independent communal resistance as long as they possess the strength and resources to launch an assault on the oppressive institutions they are resisting. However, according to Castells, these identities resist and hardly ever communicate with the state, except to struggle, negotiate, and bargain on behalf of their specific interests and values, to grant vital services to their constituencies. Castells concludes that communal (resistance) identity seems appealing to people resisting social, economic, cultural, and political oppression (Castells 1998: 356).[34]

According to Castells, project identity is constructed 'when social actors, on the basis of whichever cultural materials available to them, build a new identity that redefines their position in society, and by doing so, seek the transformation of overall social structure' (Castells 1998: 8). He explains, conceptually, how this process might take place, especially when social movements might acquire a leading role in the founding of a better society, a good life, and a good political order. In that case, the construction of identity is conducive to the realisation of a social movement's project. Although its project might originate from or be based upon an oppressed identity, it aims at the construction and the subsequent transformation of society as an extension of this project identity on the basis of communal resistance (1998: 10, 12), thus, leading to a shared, reconstructed identity.

Cultural Politics: Resisting Publics and Music

Thompson offers insights into the role of the media in ideological mobilisation in modern societies. Media reach mass audiences, and are based upon 'quasi-interaction', that is, audiences cannot answer back in a direct way (Thompson 1994: 24-37). Habermas also argues that ideology is tied to communication that is 'systematically distorted' by the exercise of domination (Habermas 1987: 120). Being cognisant of Nooshin's assertion that, 'if music's presence is an indicator of agency, then its absence is often taken to represent the opposite' (2009: 7), we might argue that in an endeavour to erase its alleged 'terrorist' image, Hizbullah exploits its media in this way. Although the Taliban exploit media and publicity differently, both Hizbullah and the Taliban can be considered as resisting publics, that is, as a counter cultural identity against the hegemonic power and lack of its legitimacy—in Hizbullah's case, against the hegemony and lack of legitimacy of the state and its institutions (Alagha 2009: 457-487), and in the Taliban's case, against foreign intervention and invasions.

Both the Taliban and Hizbullah seek to construe the world in a better way 'by listening to voices silenced by power—the voices [...] of oppressed ethnic minorities' (Goldstein 2003: 6) or subaltern voices, who, as downtrodden people, find a sense of collective identity, which lead them to mobilise in order to redress their grievances. These subaltern voices and downtrodden people are in fact the Taliban's and Hizbullah's constituency; both are empowered through an efficient application of resource mobilisation. They do this by 'music'. Overall, Hizbullah's *anashid*s and the Taliban's *tarana*s portray both as resisting publics.

Hizbullah is more assertive than the Taliban in this because of a long standing tradition in Shi'ite collective identity as being marginalised, disenfranchised, and treated as second or third class citizens. Similarly, under foreign invasions,[35] the Taliban suffered from deprivation and marginalisation—they were downtrodden, dis-enfranchised, under-represented politically, and economically deprived. Through their resistance identity, both the Taliban and Hizbullah were able to alter their miserable conditions to the better. As I will try to demonstrate later on, because of their different agendas, the Taliban affirm their resistance identity, while Hizbullah pursues the trajectory of project identity.

Taliban's *Taranas* and Hizbullah's *Anashid*

In order to illustrate the theme of jihad with music, in this section, I offer three Taliban *taranas* and compare these thematically with Hizbullah's *anashids*. I start with a point-by-point analysis whereby I offer a conceptual analysis after comparing every pair of chants.

When the Taliban were in power, they imposed a form of chanting, *taranas*, which they regard as permissible. They did not ban all musical instruments since the frame drum was considered permissible (*halal*) by them as it is sanctioned by the Prophetic tradition. Baily mentions that:

> The Taliban imposed an extreme form of music censorship, including banning the making, owning and playing of all types of musical instrument [sic] other than the frame drum [...] Unaccompanied singing does not, according to their definition, constitute music [...] they allowed various types of unaccompanied religious singing, and created a new genre, the Taliban *tarana* (lit. "song"/"chant"). The texts of these songs were usually in Pashto [...] and made frequent reference to the Taliban, their commitment to Islam, their readiness to sacrifice themselves for their country and their martyrs (*shahid*) who had died for the cause... these songs were like Pashtun folk music, but with new texts and no musical instruments and therefore "not music" (Baily 2009: 155-157).

As mentioned above, the Taliban invented a new genre of chanting, mainly based upon Pashtu folk songs and poems. Unaccompanied singing—conveyed in the form of *taranas* (chants) or *anashid* from audio cassettes—these were the only types of 'music', without instruments, allowed by the Taliban. Most of the *taranas* portray the theme of jihad with music by praising the *mujahidine*'s willingness to 'martyr' themselves for their country 'and eulogises several Taliban who have died for the cause' (Korpe 2004: 226ff). Here is the text of the first track—a *tarana*, a local 1998 production by an unknown artist—included in the accompanying CD of *Shoot the Singer* praising one such 'martyr' (*shahid*) by the name of Mudabar Jana. Its religious mobilisation purpose has been to honour and recognise the sacrifice of the one who gave his life as well as to encourage others to follow his path.

Taliban: Mudabar Jana

Greetings to you Mudabar Jana[36]
You created memories
You wrote histories
You created (inaudible)
You created (inaudible)
Your activities will be remembered everywhere and forever
Greetings to you Mudabar Jana

You created a good name for the Talibans
You created a good name for the *khadims* (servants of Allah)
You created a good name for the Muslims
You are one of the stars guiding the Taliban
Greetings to you Mudabar Jana

You annoyed the atheists
You annoyed the nonbelievers
You annoyed the bad people
You were on the right path of Allah
Greetings to you Mudabar Jana

You died for (the sake of) good people
You died for the Qur'an
You died for the name of Islam and honour
Greetings to you Mudabar Jana

You were with the Muslims
You were with the innocent

You were with the Afghanis
You were with the religious scholars
Children and aged are crying for you

You were the owner of humanity
You were the owner of nobility
You were the owner of brevity
You had love and affection in your heart
Greetings to you Mudabar Jana

You wanted to establish *Shari'a*
You wanted to establish unity
You wanted to have your own place
And you were loved by everyone (because of these views)
Greetings to you Mudabar Jana

Everyone is praising you
You had good deeds
You had good memories
We cannot find the words to praise you
Greetings to you Mudabar Jana

Similarly, Hizbullah values sacrifice in the battlefield for the service of Islam in the way of God (*fi sabili Allah*). As propaganda material, Hizbullah's music band's website[37] boasts that in 1985, *Firqat al-Wilaya* started to promote revolutionary *anashids* using rudimentary musical instruments until it evolved in 2003 into an orchestra of more than 100 musicians playing more than 40 different musical instruments, who composed symphonies that sought to deepen national sentiments and intensify human emotions. According to Hizbullah, as an effective instrument of mobilisation, *Firqat al-Wilaya* seeks in its project to accomplish a number of Islamic and humane goals. (1) develop committed art and elevate its standards in accordance with progress and revival within the religious-jurisprudential stipulations. (2) disseminate art with the purpose of developing the artistic potentials of the pious youth.

(3) adopt the choices of the oppressed, the free in their land, and propagate the spirit of the honourable Resistance in the community [Lebanon] and the *umma* [Islamic world], thus stressing human empowerment (*tamkin*).[38] (4) *Firqat al-Wilaya* remains the subaltern voice of the resistance fighters and the martyrs, spreading the fragrance of freedom in Lebanon and the *umma*.[39] As a resistance public, Hizbullah promoted mobilisation songs that extol self-sacrifice and 'martyrdom' as an empowerment mechanism in order to uphold the honour and dignity of the *umma*.

Hizbullah: Zajal[40]: Give me my Weapon[41]

Give me my weapon Oh Mother, and load the machine gun!
Hizbullah's head should remain high! (4x)

Oh precious mother, whatever happens,
I shall never let down Hizbullah (2x)

With my soul I should remain
and it has given me my pride,
with my heart and eyes and soul (2x)

Give me my weapon Oh Mother, and load the machine gun!
Hizbullah's head should remain high! (2x)

Oh Mother pray for me in your night,
so I can become a *Mujahid* [freedom fighter]
standing against *Shahyoon* (Zion) [Israel]! (3x)

So that the head of the *Umma*
can remain high and proud;
I should fight and resist with my blood
in the battle field! (2x)
Give me my weapon Oh Mother, and load the machine gun!
Hizbullah's head should remain high! (2x)

Oh Mother I am revolting against
the oppressors so that I can free the
land of my country from these enemies! (2x)
Inshallah [God willing] I will be granted Martyrdom
In this battlefield so that my path and
blood will remain a light! (2x)

Give me my weapon Oh Mother, and load the machine gun!
Hizbullah's head should remain high! (2x)

Oh precious mother, whatever happens,
I shall never let down Hizbullah (2x)

With my soul I should remain
and it has given me pride,
with my heart and eyes and soul (2x)

Give me my weapon Oh Mother, and load the machine gun!
Hizbullah's head should remain high! (2x)

The above illustrate that both the Taliban and Hizbullah highly value and praise the concepts of pride, dignity, and honour. Since Hizbullah labels itself as an Islamic *jihadi* movement, symbolic capital acquires vital importance. According to Kane, "Symbolic capital refers here to the status of a fighter for the cause of 'true Islam' whatever that means. The Koranic verse [4:95]..., which states that "God hath granted a grade higher to those who strive and fight with their goods and persons" conveys this idea of symbolic capital. The more one fights with one's 'goods' or 'one's person', the more one accumulates symbolic capital"[42] (Kane 2003: 22).

By the same token, symbolic capital is very important for the ethnic Pashtus who make up the Taliban. *Nang*, or honour, is the driving force that guides the Taliban behaviour. As such, they share the same slogan of Hizbullah: "Death is the opposite of humiliation, and death to humiliation." This attitude encourages the Taliban to engage in 'martyrdom' operations as a collective responsibility to fend off aggressors, the invading armies. While the Shi'ite call is historically grounded in Imam Husayn's call in Karbala': 'Death to humiliation' (*hayhat minna al-dhilla*), the Taliban's call does not invoke the same Shi'ite ritual; rather, it echoes a similar framework whereby the oppressed, downtrodden marginalized masses face the oppressors in order to change their lot and establish justice, and remove 'corruption in the land' (30:41) (Sarafraz 2008: 123-125). Revolutionary Islamic movements, like the Taliban and Hizbullah, employ their resource mobilisation for the aim of achieving social justice as the corner stone of an equitable society. This could only be achieved after ridding their countries of occupation and penetration, as the Taliban's *Ghazy* chant and Hizbullah's anthem illustrate.

Taliban: *Ghazy*[43]

He lives far in the high impenetrably [sic: impenetrable] mountains, our beloved *Ghazy*
Brave, honoured, heroic, and well-respected is my *Ghazy* (2x)

He is my heart, my love my beloved *Ghazy*
He is so enlighten[ed] and in love with Islam [*din*: religion] our brave *Ghazy* (2x)

He lives far in the high impenetrably mountains, our beloved *Ghazy*
Brave, honoured, heroic, and well-respected is my *Ghazy* (2x)

This is the land of Islam and honour, ready is he to give sacrifice
The pride and honour gain more and more strength in him (2x)

He lives far in the high impenetrably mountains, our beloved *Ghazy*
Brave, honoured, heroic, and well-respected is my *Ghazy* (2x)

For an Islamic Emirate in Pakistan he will shed his blood
A life like a rose, he wants to poison for the sake of Allah[44] (2x)
He lives far in the high impenetrably mountains, our beloved *Ghazy*
Brave, honoured, heroic, and well-respected is my *Ghazy* (2x)

Beloved are [sic: is] to him *Hoor al-ayn* [Their leader: 'free eye'], he wants in anyway martyrdom [sic: he's seeking martyrdom, come what may]
He is in love with freedom may Allah protect him (2x)
He lives far in the high impenetrably mountains, our beloved *Ghazy*
Brave, honoured, heroic, and well-respected is my *Ghazy* (2x)

Proud and honourable alike a lion
A lion and brave warrior is my *Ghazy*[45] (2x)
He lives far in the high impenetrably mountains, our beloved *Ghazy*
Brave, honoured, heroic, and well-respected is my *Ghazy* (2x)

Hizbullah's 1985 Anthem[46]

We walked to victory in the day of struggle, heeding up to our wounds (2x)
The wounds are chanting the gifts of heaven, the hand of God gave us weapons (2x)
And we continue on the guidance of our Qur'an, "Lo! The Party of God Is Victorious" (5: 56) (2x)

We are not only crying from freedom, we are not only defying time (2x)
We are following the unequivocal righteous path, which grants us victory after victory (2x)
And we continue on the guidance of our Qur'an, "Lo! The Party of God Is Victorious" (5: 56) (2x)

God Almighty is directing our bullets, we're going to chastise you, Israel (2x)
Our belief granted us the virtue of salvation, and from its purity we took the [Prophet's] mantle[47]
And we continue on the guidance of our Qur'an, "Lo! The Party of God Is Victorious" (5: 56) (2x)
Heaven has revealed to us the unequivocal message, which guided us through the years [whirlwind of change] (2x)
We will prevail over the aggressors, and force them to capitulate (2x)
And we continue on the guidance of our Qur'an, "Lo! The Party of God Is Victorious" (5: 56) (2x)

We will steadfastly remain [standing high], and we're going to wipe out our enemies with our bodies and souls, which always aspire to martyrdom (2x)
We're rightly guided, our souls will return to God when we die (2x)
And we continue on the guidance of our Qur'an, "Lo! The Party of God Is Victorious" (5:56) (2x)

We walked to victory in the day of struggle, heeding up to our wounds (2x)
The wounds are chanting the gifts of heaven, the hand of God gave us weapons (2x)
And we continue on the guidance of our Qur'an, "Lo! The Party of God Is Victorious" (5:56) (2x)

This calls for a short comment. The Taliban label their freedom fighter (*mujahid*), a '*Ghazy*'. This usage has an important religious connotation. In Islam, the Prophet is the *Ghazy*. He is reported to have said when he returned from some battles (*ghazawat*, singular of *ghazwa*): 'We returned from the smaller *jihad* (*al-jihad al-asghar*) and we still have [to conduct] the greater *jihad* (*al-jihad al-akbar*)'. When he was asked, what is the greater *jihad*? He replied: 'the struggle with the self (*jihad al-nafs*)'. When the Prophet participated in a battle, it was called a *ghazwa*; when he did not, it was called a *sariyya*, singular of *saraya*. Calling their *mujahid* a '*Ghazy*' is an indication of the importance of the Taliban's religious capital to mobilise; as if each *mujahid* is the 'Prophet' on conquest. This is the imagery the *mujahidin* have when they go to war (*jihad*). Hizbullah does not extend its religious capital this far; it contents itself with *al-Saraya* and does not employ '*Ghazy*'. As such, it labels its fighting force as the 'Islamic Resistance' or the 'Lebanese Brigades for Fighting the Israeli Occupation' (*Al-Saraya Al-Lubnaniyya Li-Muqawamat Al-Ihtilal Al-Israeli*). Although Hizbullah's terminology is a bit watered down in comparison to the Taliban, both chants extol the rewards of jihad as martyrdom (of the self) and victory (for the *umma*), in line with the Qur'anic verse (9:52). These themes are reiterated in the last pair of chants.

Taliban: *Mujahedeen* in Battle[48]

In afar in the black mountains there is cracking and whizzing of bullets,

The mujahedeen are in view
Attack on the Campaign (Military Base) is ongoing afar in the black mountains (2x)

Sand, dusty [sic: dust] and the black smoke and red flames
Look [at] the situation [condition] of our village[49], coloured with red blood (2x)

In afar in the black mountains there is cracking and whizzing of bullets,
The mujahedeen are in view
Attack on the Campaign (Military Base) is ongoing afar in the black mountains (2x)
In the air the infidels' aircrafts are flying by, raining bombs on us
Look at our martyred village[50], it is ravaged devastated with bombs (2x)

In afar in the black mountains there is cracking and whizzing of bullets,
The mujahedeen are in view
Attack on the Campaign (Military Base) is ongoing afar in the black mountains (2x)

Youngs [The young] were filled with honour, elders have also come out
Everyone has taken his military equipment [arms, weapons] from the early times (2x)

In afar in the black mountains there is cracking and whizzing of bullets,
The mujahedeen are in view
Attack on the Campaign (Military Base) is ongoing afar in the black mountains (2x)

Oh Allah assist them, like you assist Hasfiz Naser, They have come out for the sake of you (Oh Allah)
They have defended with honour your religion (Oh Allah) (2x)

In afar in the black mountains there is cracking and whizzing of bullets,
The mujahedeen are in view
Attack on the Campaign (Military Base) is ongoing afar in the black mountains (2x)

Hizbullah: *Nashid*: Oh Imam Husayn we are the Nation of Hizbullah[51]

Oh Imam Husayn we are Hizbullah's nation (2x)
In the footsteps of Imam Khumayni we march, in the way of God (*fi sabili Allah*)
In the footsteps of Imam Khamina'i we march, in the way of God (2x)

We do not bow down, save to God Almighty
We fear neither the tyrants nor the lashes of the whip
We are infatuated with martyrdom in the way of God (2x)

Oh Imam Husayn we are Hizbullah's nation (2x)
In the footsteps of Imam Khumayni we march, in the way of God
In the footsteps of Imam Khamina'i we march, in the way of God (2x)

Oh Husayn's heart, you were overcoming, oh how much you were burdened
And you struggled with fortitude, delineating the path of glory
We are infatuated with martyrdom in the way of God (2x)

Oh Imam Husayn we are Hizbullah's nation (2x)
In the footsteps of Imam Khumayni we march, in the way of God
In the footsteps of Imam Khamina'i we march, in the way of God (2x)

We extend our allegiance, fidelity, and immolation to you, Imam Husayn
We will not wane or be weakened, and we'll remain adamant in the face of the enemies
We sacrifice ourselves to you, to the pure belief, to the belief of the Sayyids[52]
We are infatuated with martyrdom in the way of God (2x)

Oh Imam Husayn we are Hizbullah's nation (2x)
In the footsteps of Imam Khumayni we march, in the way of God
In the footsteps of Imam Khamina'i we march, in the way of God (2x)

We do not bow down, save to God Almighty
We fear neither the tyrants nor the lashes of the whip

We will remain revolutionaries until we liberate our occupied land
We are infatuated with martyrdom in the way of God (2x)

Although the Taliban forbade music *per se*, the chants above reveal a considerable dimension of the Taliban's employment of jihad with 'music', which in terms of themes, content, and purpose, that is, mobilisation seem similar to Hizbullah's *anashid*. This analysis leads us to delve into the Taliban's and Hizbullah's views on music behind these chants and *anashid* in order to construe the justifications each party gives for engaging in such behaviour.

Taliban's Views on Music

Unlike Hizbullah, the Taliban do not have elaborate views on music *per se*, rather edicts and prohibitions censuring music, musicians, and musical instruments.

The Taliban's Edicts Banning Music and Musical Instruments

Overall, the Taliban consider music as: 'an abomination of the Devil [*rigsun min 'mal al-Shaytan*]', as a specific interpretation of the Qur'anic verse (5:90): "O believers, wine, gambling, idols and divining arrows are an abomination of the Devil's doing; so avoid them that perchance you may prosper!" Further, they construe the Qur'anic verse (31:6) as a ban on music and singing: "There are some people who purchase idle talk [*lahu al-hadith*] in order to lead away from Allah's path without any knowledge; and take it in jest. Those will have a demeaning punishment." More specifically, the Taliban interpret '*lahu al-hadith*' as singing and listening to musical instruments that distract from praying and invoking God (Baig 2008: 105-166). By 1998, the Taliban succeeded in completely forbidding music and musical instruments (save the frame drum) in Afghanistan (Malm 2008: 9, 57, 61). They were known for their strict rulings of imposing Islamic penal law (*hudud*[53]).

The Taliban released decrees/edicts related to cultural issues, especially music, where their Islamic cultural sphere was supposed to be void of such a practice. Under the Qur'anic injunction of 'enjoining the good and forbidding the evil' (which is also the name of their religious police) (Sarafraz 2008: 134-140), and out of concern of imposing Islamic ethics in line with the stipulations of Islamic law (*Shari'a*), in December 1996, the Taliban issued and enforced various decrees with regard to music right up until they were forced out of power in 2001:

> To prevent music to be broadcasted by the public information resources. In shops, hotels, vehicles and rickshaws cassettes, and music are prohibited. This matter should be monitored within five days. If any music cassette found in a shop, the shopkeeper should be imprisoned and the shop locked. If five people guarantee the shop should be opened the criminal released later. If cassette found in the vehicle, the vehicle and the driver will be imprisoned. If five people guarantee the vehicle will be released and the criminal released later (Rashid 2008: 218).

The Taliban also banned music in weddings and playing the drum, stipulations that run contrary to the Prophetic tradition that sanctioned music at festive occasions[54] such as the celebrations of the end of fasting during the holy month of *Ramadan* (*'Id al-Fitar*) and Abraham's feast of sacrifice (*'Id al-Adha*) and weddings. They might have done it out of fear of the power of music in corrupting the soul, as Baig (2008: 93, 105) and the following edicts seem to suggest:

> To prevent music and dances in wedding parties. In the case of violation, the head of the family will be arrested and punished.
> To prevent the playing of the music drum. This prohibition should be announced. If anybody does this then the religious elders will decide about it (Rashid 2008: 218-219).

Bearing in mind that no 'pious entertainment' was allowed, public burning of musical instruments as well as subjecting those who breach their edicts on audio and visual music to *hudud* testify to the Taliban's extreme puritanical measures (Rashid 2008; Kopke 2004: 19-28).

All musical instruments were banned, and when discovered by agents of the Office for the Propagation of Virtue and the Prevention of Vice were destroyed, sometimes being burnt in public along with confiscated audio and video cassettes, TV sets and VCRs (all visual representation of animate beings is also prohibited)...Taliban rejection of the visual representation of animate beings, whether human or animal, leads to the rejection of all forms of visual media such as cinema, television, video, family photographs and representational painting. And the Taliban have banned music... the Taliban are simply extremely puritanical and against any form of enjoyment or entertainment outside the sphere of religion (Baily 2001: 7, 35, 41, 42-3; Cf. Sarafraz 2008, 139).

Is it the case that the debate on music is actually part of the chronic debate on the interpretation of religious texts? For the Taliban, the matter is settled finally on the side of prohibitions in the absolute.

As argued before, Khalid Baig seems not only to be a mere sympathiser of the Taliban's doctrines, causes, and views on music, but also could be labelled as an intellectual defender of the Taliban because he seems to vindicate and exonerate them, as if he is suggesting that their version of Islam is the only 'right' and 'authentic' one (Baig 2008: 262, n. 11). Baig gives the impression that the West fought and ousted the Taliban because of their views on music. He writes, "The Taliban succeeded in banning music as long as they ruled. It is probably an indication of their resilience that unlike the Iranian revolution the Taliban revolution was not expected to crumble on its own. They had to be bombed out[55] [...] The murder and mayhem caused by that [US-led] invasion thus appeared to be an appropriate punishment for the crime of banning music [...] and film."[56] Concerning *Le Monde*'s report 'that the Taliban had asked the people to free their captive birds to keep them from listening to their singing',[57] Baig vehemently goes to their defence claiming, "What the Taliban has been concerned about was the captivity of the poor birds and not their singing!" How could that be when one of the Taliban's edicts stipulates the killing of birds for two main reasons—(1) fear of being enchanted by listening to their singing (*tarab*); and (2) amusement or idle pastime, which the Taliban regard as a diversion from prayer (*lahu*) in line with their selective interpretation of the Qur'anic verse (31:6), as Baig concedes.[58]

Baig makes the case for the Taliban by arguing against the following four notions:—(1) jihad with music; (2) purposeful art; (3) pious fun and entertainment; and (4) the use of music for Islamic propagation. First, he criticises the use of music in *jihad*, contending that singing cannot be an act of worship of Allah.[59] Although Baig regards jihad with music, or music for mobilisation purposes and war effort, as un-Islamic, he concedes that music's 'effect in exciting soldiers on the battlefield is undeniable'.[60] He adds that 'singing was an act of worship' for the Pakistani army, which was indoctrinated on the triad of belief, piety, and *jihad*.[61] According to Baig, "The music is filled with devilish messages of violence, sex, drugs, and defiance of all authority that are corrupting the young minds of the planet earth,"[62] he does not support the idea that 'good music' is needed to drive out 'bad music'.[63] Second, purposeful art does not exist in his view. He writes, "A lot of what is offered today in 'Islamic' concerts or through music recordings is a weapon of mass distraction, although it may create illusions of virtue."[64] Third, as he repeatedly stated, 'pious fun and entertainment' are not sanctioned; both are prohibited in the absolute.[65] Finally, he condemns the use of music for Islamic propagation and charity, arguing that 'The message of Islam is a very serious message'.[66] In this regard, Baig lashes Yusuf Islam (Cat Stevens) stressing that his justifications for returning to music after almost three decades of giving it up were 'slick nothings based on commonly held misconceptions'.[67] Thus, Baig accuses Yusuf Islam of practicing 'self-gratification', rather than Islamic charity, 'which is giving in the path of Allah'.[68] At the end of the book, Baig comes to the unsubstantiated conclusion that there exists almost unanimity among the religious scholars (*'ulama'*) to ban music: "Most music is prohibited by a near consensus of scholars...in all generations prominent scholars have condemned music in no uncertain terms."[69]

This is quite different from Hizbullah's 'theory on music' that sanctions almost all of the Taliban's prohibitions above within certain religious safeguards (*al-mahadhir al-shar'iyya*) that respect the religious sensibilities of the audience, so as not to deflect from their intended noble purpose, and thus, degenerate into lowbrow art (*al-fann al-habit*).

Hizbullah's Views on Music

Compared to the Taliban's list of prohibitions, Hizbullah seems to have elaborate views on music, to the extent that the Party claims these views constitute a 'music theory'. However, in comparison to Western theories on music, Hizbullah's views seem rudimentary. The paragraph below is from the introduction to Hizbullah's so-called 'music theory', as posted on its music band's website:

> Revolution is also a language that caters to a special kind of human emotions and feelings that are expressed by dignity, honour, advancement, and Islamic revival or renaissance (*nuhud*)[70]. Rhetorically, revolution is always an awakening, a stimulation that comes at a time when one of the human languages stutters. Metaphorically, art and revolution are languages that coalesce and live within the human being; when one wakes up, the other ensues. When the time was ripe for action and resistance, it was inevitable for the language of art to appear on the scene and to accompany this revolution, this new eventuality in order to satisfy an urgent need, the need of intellectual pleasures at a time when many people were engaged in vices and 'corruption in the land' (7:176) leading a life of degeneration and diversion into sensual pleasures.[71]

Unlike the Taliban, Hizbullah values revolutionary art, and practices resistance art as a manifestation of art in the service of 'noble human goals'. Unlike the Taliban, Hizbullah favours jihad with music, encourages the use of music in supplication (*du'a*), and promotes 'fun' or pious entertainment, leisure time and recreational activities.

Ideology (Revolution) and Art

Hizbullah's so-called 'music theory' considers art as a language that addresses human emotions and feelings.[72] The head of Media Relations, Sayyid Ibrahim al-Musawi,[73] clarifies that the Islamic perspective on art is holistic, deep, and committed towards the realisation of 'noble aims'. Al-Musawi observes that *inshad* (chanting) and music are present in all the natural manifestations of the world—in the sound of the wind, the leaves, the rain, the waves, the birds, etc. According to him, "1000 symphonies are not worth the singing of a little bird." Al-Musawi refers to the prophets of the Old Testament, or for that matter the Qur'an: "David had the gift of song and sacred music, and this is shown in the Psalms. All nature—hills and birds –sing and echo back the praises of God' (Yusuf 'Ali 1993: 1136) [...] and Solomon commanded the wind: (34:10): 'We bestowed Grace aforetime on David from ourselves: 'O ye Mountains! Sing ye back the Praises of Allah with him! and ye birds (also)!'...(34:12): 'And to Solomon (We made) the Wind (obedient) [...]' According to al-Musawi, this great empowerment and command over the forces of nature, which David and Solomon were endowed with by God, were all for the sake of singing praises to the Lord through the things He had created. Al-Musawi considers chanting and music in the service of accomplishing the primary goal of achieving God's will in this world in disseminating goodness, justice, love, and peace to humanity at large. According to him, the aforementioned are the components of resistance art: purposeful, committed art with a mission. Al-Musawi views Hizbullah's understanding and employment of music and *anashid* within this framework, which serves the ultimate goal: committed art with worth and purpose. He concludes that resistance art 'elevates human worth and raises the soul to its highest perfection to achieve the highest stance that God willed to man'.

Shaykh Shafiq Jaradi, the Rector of *Al-Ma'arif Al-Hikmiyya* College, acknowledged that the existence of a 'music theory' in Islam implies that it is permissible (*halal*) to discuss the issue of legitimacy of music. He adds that there is no music theory in Islam in the absolute; rather, it is based on the Muslims' social practice and their understanding of Islam and the religious texts. He clarifies that in the texts, there are no clear features of a music school; rather indications that portray the legitimacy and sanctioning of music (*hulliyya*) from two main perspectives: (1) Islamic civilisation, and (2) the experiences of Muslim religious scholars *('ulama)*.

According to Jaradi, music constitutes part of the world of art, the world of sensations, passions, and spirituality. However, every artist erects her/his own spiritual world based on her/his preconceived ideas. Therefore, the personification of every artwork depends on the individual, on the artist himself. Concerning the 'centrality of the Word', Jaradi questions: are there similar features and frameworks among the artists' sensibilities to the extent of basing a music theory on these? The centrality of the embodiment of beauty (*tajalli*) in Islam is the Word, whether it is the wisdom of a hadith or a Qur'anic verse. Jaradi adds that the Qur'an has its own special music (*tajwid* and *talhin*). The Qur'an encouraged tolerance and preached how to deal with the word and execute it. For instance, supplication (*du'a'*) is the propagation of words that portray its own standards in music's significance and meaning. Jaradi continues noting that music is also rhythm. The more the rhythm is in line with the words, the more is the likelihood of extracting a music theory. The more the words and rhythm are coalescent and integrated, and the more the rhythm adds to the intonation of words, the more we speed up the process of propagating a music theory in Islam. Words render legitimacy and rhythm too. However, Shaykh Jaradi acknowledges that this requires extensive research on the relationship between the words, on the one hand, and the experiences of the Islamic civilisation, on the other.

In conclusion, Shaykh Jaradi concedes that there are no promulgated standing rules (specific rules) that we can extract from a specific music theory in Islam. Rather, we can lay down its framework and read its contours in the Shi'ite tradition based on recent developments, that is, the experiences of the Islamic Republic of Iran and those of Hizbullah, for instance.[74]

Employing a meta-philosophical, jurisprudential discourse and approach in laying out a 'music theory' in Islam, Shaykh Akram Barakat, the head of the *Cultural Islamic Al-Ma'arif Association* argues that Hizbullah's view towards art is not static; rather dynamic and evolutionary as time elapses. In this regard, it is worth clarifying that the Shi'ites have to emulate (follow the religious rulings) of a living religious authority (*marja'*) who is conversant with current developments.[75]

MP 'Ali Fayyad told me that historically music and singing were banned because they were in the service of carnal and moral vices and debaucheries (*fawahish*).[76] According to him, now things have changed. Music has become a realistic, noble, and humanistic endeavour addressing the values of beauty and goodness.As he noted, the change of the function and purpose of music, eventually changes prohibition to acceptance. Thus, one ought to engage positively and constructively in purposeful, mobilisation art in order to fend off debaucheries and inculcate Islamic values and norms.[77]

Employing a social anthropological approach, Hajj Muhammad Ra'd, the current head of Hizbullah's parliamentary bloc and *Shura* Council member, argued that the Prophet chose Bilal, the black slave, to perform the call of prayer (*adhan*) simply because he had a beautiful voice that could stimulate human emotions in a purposeful-positive way. According to Ra'd, Bilal combined a beautiful voice with a solid performance and presence as the epitome of spirituality. The music of the Qur'an is the music of the soul: this is the meaning of *tajwid* according to Ra'd. *Tajwid* personifies the commitment to the rules of reciting; it is the embodiment of the word with music. The Prophet used to tell him: '*arihna ya Bilal* [relieve us Bilal]' in reference to asking him to perform the call of prayer. Ra'd added that the Prophet admonished '*rattil al-Qur'an tartilan* [recite the Qur'an in the manner of hymns]'. Ra'd defined *tartil* as creativity in the projection of sound waves or producing guttural, pharyngeal sounds in a skilful way from the throat (vocal cords). Like Jaradi, Ra'd notes the importance of the word and its fusion with rhythm: the more legible the word is, the more powerful is the message, the higher the effect of music. This is the way, jihad with music, is performed by Hizbullah as a purposeful committed art, as a resistance art.[78]

According to MP 'Ali Fayyad, Iran played a leading role in reforming the classical understanding of music, and Hizbullah followed suit in abiding by Imam Khamina'i's jurisprudential understanding of music: "There is nothing intrinsically prohibited in music in itself." Rather, it has to do with who consumes it and for what purpose. Thus, the nature of the listener and his way of interaction with music determines *haram* (prohibition) or *halal* (permission), in addition to the content and subject matter of the music. From the perspective of resistance art, music invokes the feelings of beauty, goodness, the intellectual love of God, and evokes nostalgia towards the homeland and its people. Opposed to that is lowbrow art that promotes vices, hatred, isolation, and the likes; as such, this type of music is *haram*.[79]

Jihad with Music and Resistance Art

Hajj Ghalib Abu Zaynab, Hizbullah's officer for Muslim-Christian dialogue, defines resistance art as social art, as a positive art. According to him, resistance art concentrates on just rhythm and poetic words that deal with people's humanistic and social causes, aimed at polishing and sharpening potential skills. From this perspective, it is labelled as positive art. According to him, resistance art promotes ethical and spiritual beauty and stresses the concept of God's mercy. Abu Zaynab adds that Resistance is a positive act: resisting oppression and crying for freedom are legitimate in order to rectify the present imbalance, but with temperance as Prophet Muhammad has enjoined: "You are the *umma* of moderation (*wasatiyya*)." According to him, moderation in life is the standard norm and value that we ought to follow, as it is the precept of practice of the Prophetic tradition. Resistance is a social reflection to the ills rupturing the moral fibre of the community. In response to my question of why Hizbullah stresses so much the concept of social justice in its *anashid*, Abu Zaynab stressed that the purpose of resistance art is to do away with oppression and with all the ills that society faced in terms of derailing and deflecting it towards delinquency and aggression. Resistance art aims at promoting justice, meritocracy, integrity, and philanthropy. Resistance art is not alien to society; rather it is part and parcel of it. It expresses the will of society and addresses people's sensibilities and emotions. Resistance art is an embodiment of greater jihad, societal jihad, the jihad against the self and its corrupt desires. Abu Zaynab states that resistance art contributes to the development of society in a positive way, thus guiding society away 'from darkness (evil) into light (virtues) by reforming the self and morals'. He concludes that the evidence that resistance art is of a refined calibre is its employment in Hizbullah's media institutions and the Islamic Republic of Iran's cultural activities.[80]

According to Muhammad Kawtharani, the vice-president of Hizbullah's Cultural Unit, the role of 'resistance art' lies in the conversion of the elements of power and realizing them in Hizbullah's 'resistance society'. He defines resistance art as the art of Islamic revival or renaissance (*nuhud*) that revitalises the *umma* and wakes it up from its hibernation. It is the art that moves emotions and feelings to struggle against invasion, occupation, and oppression. In line with Hizbullah's resource mobilisation, this cultural resistance puts the Party's artistic capabilities to the test through promoting resistance art that chants purposeful words balanced by beautiful rhythms and intonations (personal interview, August 07, 2009).

Concerning the artistic frameworks, Kawtharani clarified that Hizbullah's 2003 founded 'The Lebanese Association of Arts' (*Risalat*) follows the Islamic historical message. By way of an example in relation to music, he asserted that in the domain of expressing Islamic values, Islamic culture was more inclined towards chanting (*inshad*) rather than listening to musical instruments. [In this regard, Crete attributes this phenomenon to the saliency of *adhan* (call of prayer) over music in Islamic culture, while she noted the opposite trend in Western countries due to the influence of church music (Crete 2008)]. Like Ra'd, he argues that primacy was given to the Word, rather than music as such. Benefiting from such an experience and expanding it to a pragmatic attempt to construct an 'alternative modernity' that balances between (1) musical instruments, playing, composing, and compiling music, on the one hand, and (2) the chanted word, on the other. This is what the artistic framework sanctions in relation to the message that aims to provoke change while upholding Islamic authenticity (values, norms) (Sbayti, February 15, 2010).

'Fun' or Pious Entertainment: Leisure Time and Recreational Activities

MP 'Ali Fayyad comes out with an important taxonomy whereby enchantment (*tarab*)[81] implies negative relaxation, idleness (*istirkha'*), while *anashid* imply vigilance (*hamas*). The subject matter of *anashid* deals with the right to defend the homeland, the country, and extols 'martyrdom'. Fayyad clarifies that Hizbullah sanctions 'fun' or pious entertainment, but not seduction (*ighwa'*) and debaucheries.[82] Within this framework, Shaykh Akram Barakat stresses the need for leisure time and recreational activities since these are vital to man's well-being and productivity. Good upbringing fortifies the human being from outside pollution such as vices, seduction, and debaucheries. Imam 'Ali has noted that the animal was created with desire without reason (*'aql*); the angels were endowed with reason, but not desires; while the human being was created having both reason and desire. Imam 'Ali stressed that reason can elevate man to a higher stance than the angels, while desire can demote him to a lower level than an animal. Thus, the struggle in man between reason and desire should always give primacy to reason, as Shi'ite jurisprudence dictates. The Shi'ites believe that jurisprudence should adhere to intellectual foundations. Everything that the human being receives should be in line with his/her coalescence (*takamul*) aiming at elevating him/her higher. This is the Islamic vision that Hizbullah believes in regarding art, music, *anashid*, etc. From this perspective, resistance art and jihad with music are practiced. Shaykh Barakat considers chanting (*al-inshad*) an artistic jihad (*jihad fanni*), cultural jihad whereby man's chanting and playing of musical instruments draws him closer to God. Shaykh Barakat stressed that Shi'ite jurisprudence fuses/moulds religion in all aspects of life.[83]

Shaykh Barakat argues that Hizbullah's call in the realm of culture and art is to fill people's leisure time with purposeful artistic activities that promote high ethical stands that are conducive to elevating the moral worth of man. According to Barakat, Hizbullah always looks for balanced alternatives, knowing that the self ceases to produce while it is engaged in constant effort. Man needs rest and recreational activities that are part of the growth of the human being from the perspective of piety, in his aspiration, to come closer to God. To reach that purpose man has to sleep, rest, in order to perform prayer and jihad: "The sleeping of the jurist is better than the prayer of the ignorant (*nawn al-'alim khayrun min salat al-jahil*)." We should always look up to our purpose: sleep is important in order for the human being to be able to perform the duties of prayer and jihad. Shaykh Barakat reiterates: "It all has to do with the issue of purposefulness (*al-hadafiyya*),"[84] and therein lies the main juncture of resistance art.

From Theory to Practice: Hizbullah and the Taliban

Although Hizbullah portrays a specific understanding of resistance art to the extent of proposing a 'music theory' in Islam, the Party's views on music seem to be backed by practice. On the other hand, there seem to be gaps between the Taliban's views on music and actual practice, since the stipulated prohibitions were not fully enforced, especially when it comes to *taranas*, which the Taliban do not consider 'music', as such.

In direct opposition to Hizbullah and in line with the Taliban, Khalid Baig, their seemingly intellectual defender, argues against the contribution of music to the war effort; art with a mission; controlled fun or pious entertainment; and the utilisation of music to spread the message of Islam. On the contrary, for Hizbullah singing can indeed be an act of worship of Allah. Like the Pakistani army, the Party blended belief (*iman*), piety (*taqwa*), and *jihad* with music. Music constitutes part and parcel of their identity as Shi'ites. As my interviewees have indicated, especially Shaykh Akram Barakat, Hizbullah—in line with the Shi'ite traditions—enjoins the pursuit of 'purposeful fun' within the domain of certain religious safeguards to the extent of arguing that Islam sanctions fun and enjoins disseminating happiness in the hearts of the believers, providing for those who do so a great remuneration in heaven, as Moses, the Prophet, the fifth Imam Muhammad al-Baqir, and the sixth Iman Ja'far al-Sadiq had admonished (Cultural Islamic Al-Ma'arif Association 2007: 6-7). Quite the opposite of the Taliban, Imam Khamina'i repeatedly stated that art is the most eloquent and effective means of Islamic propagation (2009: 6, 9, 27, 50, 83),[85] which constitutes the crux of Hizbullah's justification of resistance art. Khamina'i stressed that any message, or call, or revolution, or civilisation, or culture, cannot be successfully disseminated if it is not expressed in artistic form (Imam Khamina'i 2006: 147-167; 221-226).

In line with this call, Hizbullah is a strong supporter of art with a mission, and is promoting it through its weekly newspaper *al-Intiqad*; media institutions such as *al-Manar* satellite TV; *al-Nour* satellite radio; and most importantly, *Risalat*. Hizbullah is aggressively campaigning to promote its new image, it new face that supports jihad with music and resistance art, on the one hand, on par with defensive jihad, on the other, as Imam Khamina'i has called for when he attributed the term 'Greater Jihad' to the former and 'Smaller Jihad' to the latter.[86]

Hizbullah

MP Nawwaf al-Musawi, Hizbullah's leading philosopher and humanist intellectual, believes that cultural politics does not only mean integration in the political system by contesting legislative, and municipal elections and joining the council of ministers (the main executive body in Lebanon), but also artistic production could be viewed as a medium, as a public space for politicisation and struggle. According to him, the salient feature of cultural politics is the exercise of power within the narrow confines of the institutional and constitutional structures of the state, which may hinder or place limitations and restrictions on social actions and cultural practices of marginalised groups. Concerning Hizbullah's understanding of cultural citizenship, al-Musawi clarifies that the Party aims at elevating the plight of the oppressed Shi'ite masses to achieve balanced development on par with the other privileged groups that make up the 18 ethno-confessional communities in Lebanon. Thus, in its generic sense, Hizbullah views cultural citizenship as a means to rid the community of its historic social injustice, alienation, exploitation, and marginalisation by making their subaltern voices heard—not only in their quest for more equitable representation and better access to the resources of the state, but also in their struggle to boost their cultural capital[87] by exercising cultural resilience for the aim of obtaining empowerment (*tamkin*) in the long run.[88]

Since 'symbolic social meanings are shaped through relations of power' (Nooshin 2009: 10), Hizbullah embarked on altering the plight of the Lebanese Shi'ites from being marginalized and oppressed to being empowered, not only in politics but also in culture and public spaces. In addition to its integration in the Lebanese public sphere, when the Party rose to fame, Hizbullah resorted to the 'collective language' of art and music in order to convey its cultural face through 'Resistance Art' (*al-fann al-muqawim*), or 'committed art with a purpose' (*al-fann al-hadif al-multazim*).

Shaykh Na'im Qasim, Hizbullah's deputy secretary general, argues that 'jihad with music' is not only sanctioned but is also highly recommended in its capacity as a purposeful (*hadif*) mobilisation tool. He adds that pious entertainment such as purposeful, balanced and zealous *anashid* that convey virtuous content are mostly extolled as a form of resistance art that is blossoming with beautiful pictures filled with love and mobilisation.[89] Shaykh Shafiq Jaradi told me that the issue of sanctioning (*hulliyya* from *halal*) of music is taken for granted since Hizbullah propagates a form of 'music theory in Islam'.[90] Shaykh 'Ali Daher, the head of Hizbullah's Cultural Unit, refers to this trend of art as resistance art (*al-fann al-muqawim*). He explains that it branches from committed Islamic art with a mission (*al-fann al-hadif al-multazim*) but is distinguished by its content and message that deal with political and social issues as well as themes such as jihad, sacrifice, patriotism, and the like. Daher is against purposeless art (*al-fann al-'abathi*) or art for the sake of art; rather he is for purposeful art, especially chants (*anashid*) that further the cause of jihad with music. In other words, Daher regards *al-fann al-muqawim* as a specific genre of *al-fann al-hadif*, which is distinguished by its subject matter.[91]

Hizbullah's views on music are backed by practice. The Party's music groups, *Firqat al-Wilaya*, and, *Orchestra Shams al-Hurriyya*, testify to the trend of resistance art. Hizbullah's official music group *Firqat al-Wilaya*[92] was established in 1985. It composed the Party's anthem[93] and is mainly concerned with producing Islamic *anashid* (songs, hymns, and anthems) that mobilize Hizbullah's constituency to perform *jihad* against any aggressor. The women's *Firqat al-Wilaya* (*Firqat al-Wilaya al-Nisa'iyya*) followed suite and a subsidiary group *Firqat Fajr al-Isra' al-Inshadiyya* also branched from it.[94] Hizbullah is the only Islamic party to employ a full Western style orchestra. *Orchestra Shams al-Hurriyya* ('Freedom's Sun Orchestra') has been producing symphonies since its founding in 2003. It is a new endeavour to elevate purposeful music and *anashid* to the level of professionalism, as its reason d'être statement stipulates.[95] Thus, Hizbullah is a strong supporter of committed art with a purpose, and, as mentioned earlier, is promoting it through its weekly newspaper *al-Intiqad* and media institutions such as *al-Manar* satellite TV and *al-Nour* satellite radio, and most importantly 'The Lebanese Association of Arts' (*Risalat*). Founded in 2003, *Risalat* is a subsidiary non-profit organisation of Hizbullah's Cultural Unit aiming to promote resistance art as an expression of the 'culture of resistance', mainly in its audio-visual works, as its reason d'être statement stipulates.[96] This seems in line with 'the belief that music possessed moral qualities and could affect character and behaviour [...] also resonate indirectly with the long-standing debate within Islamic jurisprudence over the moral standing of music' (Nooshin 2009: 9).

Taliban

The Taliban's *taranas* seem reminiscent of the songs of cameleers (*huda'*), which are a form of singing, usually without musical instruments, which were chanted in front of caravans during the Prophet's time for the purpose and benefit (*maslaha*) of both the camels and the cameleers in order to increase the camels' pace and make them stick together. Khalid Baig, who in his book on music legitimises and defends the policies of the Taliban, acknowledges: "*Huda'* singing [which depends on the quality of the singer's voice] has been a firmly established practice in the pre-Islamic period [*jahiliyya*], and it was maintained by the Prophet, but with restrictions" (Baig 2008: 37-39).

In actual practice, the Taliban do not strictly ban 'music' since they have their own tapes and anthem, and play the frame drum (Malm 2008: 62; Freemuse 2007: 57) as some form of jihad with music. Baily argues that 'the only forms of musical expression permitted today are the singing of certain kinds of religious poetry, and so-called Taliban 'chants', which are panegyrics to Taliban principles and commemorations of those who have died on the field of battle for the Taliban cause...' (2001: 7, 9). Freemuse adds, "If from an ethno-musicological perspective we do consider Taliban *taranas* to be a form of music, it shows that when one thing is censored it is often to promote something else which is uncensored" (2007: 9).

The Taliban's stance on music censorship was not fully enforced. Based on the concept of public interest (*maslaha*), they promoted jihad with music according to the dictates of the battlefield or as a potent mobilisation tool: 'The Taliban songs or marches are songs without musical instruments. It mostly consists of national poems describing the situation or criticising the deeds of the opposition or concern stories of Jihad (the holy war against foreign invaders and their puppets). The Taliban songs are composed based on the famous Afghan songs with traditional melodies that are sold widely in Afghanistan' (Freemuse 2001: 29). Baily adds:

> The Taliban produce their own cassettes of chanting and singing, with texts in praise of themselves, often mentioning by name those who have died for the cause... Taliban-approved cassettes are invariably plastered with images of rifles and rocket-launchers. They not only promote the Taliban's prowess in the battlefield but fulfil the government injunction that the taking and displaying of pictures of living creatures is un-Islamic. These cassettes are available for purchase in the bazaar... (2001: 37).

Thus, in actual practice, it seems the Taliban did not rigorously conform to their imposed views on music censorship, conceding that there are differences between what they classify as 'music', and what we regard as music as such.

> ... the Taliban soldiers who were studying music at the Islamabad Music Institute..." It may be safe to say that the subtext to the debate about whether or not music and Islam go together is actually a disguised debate about the interpretation of the religion itself and its sacred texts (Freemuse 2007: 55).

Conclusion

This article demonstrated that both Hizbullah and the Taliban employ revolutionary 'music'—*taranas* and *anashid*—as an effective mobilisation tool that furthers the cause of *jihad* with music, which is, in turn, conducive to accumulating symbolic capital. Starting from the same Qur'anic premise of *'amal al-ihsan* (action of excellence under God's guidance), the Taliban and Hizbullah reached different conclusions due to their different readings of (what constitutes) authentic or pure Islam, on the one hand, and divergent interpretations of reality and the status quo ante, on the other. Based on this process of rationalisation and legitimisation of the good political order (Islamic sate), they devised their own views on 'music' as a medium of agency and empowerment in the process of power struggle, negotiation, and bargaining. By portraying themselves as 'resistance publics', their music become a public space for contesting, challenging, and resisting certain dominant ideologies or 'hegemons'—holders of power. The author reached the tentative conclusion that it seems that Hizbullah's views on music are backed by practice, while those of the Taliban are not; or Hizbullah seems to be more consistent than the Taliban in this regard. It appears that the Taliban banned one form of chanting to legitimise another, although they did not call it 'music' as such.

This article argued that although for the Taliban the music prohibition is in the absolute, for Hizbullah the matter is entirely different; it is contextual. Both Imam Khumayni and Khamina'i argue that there is no prohibition in the absolute on singing, music, and musical instruments; rather based on the context, content, and usage, prohibition or sanctioning is issued (Al-Hamidi 1994: 107-108). In line with Shi'ite jurisprudence, all my interviewees have accorded that the only genre that is prohibited in singing and music is the one that leads to corruption, moral vices, and debaucheries, since it is thought that desire takes control over reason rendering man an instinctual animal. Save that, everything else is sanctioned. This is in concordance with what Khumayni and Khamina'i have stipulated. Noteworthy, in Shi'ite jurisprudence, 'the ruler's ordinance abrogates the *mujtahid*'s fatwa' (*hukum al-hakim yanqud fatwa al-mujtahid*), if the societal interest (*maslaha*) requires such a course of action. For instance, earlier Shi'ite jurists (*mujtahids*) prohibited chess because it was used as an instrument of gambling. When its usage changed to an intellectual tool that promotes critical thinking, its ruling changed from prohibition (*haram*) to sanctioning (*halal*). The same ruling applies to the use of musical instruments, even if they were previously employed in the sessions of vices and corruption (*majalis al-fisq wa al-fujur*). To reiterate, according to the Hizbullah establishment, art and music are not in themselves *haram*. Things that were previously *haram* could become *halal* and vice versa. For example, reciting the Qur'an in the sessions of vices and corruption is haram; while reciting love poetry (*ghazal*) in the manner of reciting the Qur'an (*tajwid*) is *halal*. In other words, unlike the Taliban who prohibit in the absolute, for Hizbullah prohibition or sanctioning is contextual: it has to do with the variables of time, place, and environment, on the one hand, and context, content, and message (*risala*), on the other. Hizbullah stresses that what has to be kept in mind is the telos—aim, goal, or purpose. From here stems the justification of art with a purpose, art with a mission (*al-fann al-hadif*) or 'resistance art'. Shaykh Akram Barakat argues that Islam calls for progress in all domains: reform in art and music elevates human worth and values. As such, he states, 'the basis of Shi'ite jurisprudence is the call for innovation and modernity in order to be up-to-date with all aspects of life. God does not judge solely based on the results, rather the intentions (*niyyat*). This notion leaves room for jurisprudential innovations (*al-tajaddud al-fiqhi*)' (Cf. Imam Khamina'i 2004: 16-51).

Although resistance identity is the main trait that characterises a social movement, its transformation into a mainstream political party aiming at empowering society, or exercising control and hegemony on it, depends on, to which extent the social movement is capable of reconstructing its identity by upgrading its resistance identity to a project identity. Castells stresses that integration alone in the system or state structures is not sufficient for a social movement to acquire a project identity since it might content itself with negotiations, bargaining, compromise, and dealings with other actors, thus behaving like any interest group or political party that plays according to the rules of the game as set by the system. Rather, he argues, a social movement needs to *transform* the overall society to 'dominant interests enacted by global flows of capital, power, and information' (1998: 357). This seems not to be an easy task. Can Hizbullah accomplish this difficult, but not impossible task in the near future? And what about the Taliban?

Hizbullah seems to accommodate and change its identity within the guidelines of Islamic fixities/immutables (*thawabit*), and authenticity in order to accompany progress and development, thus constructively working within its humanistic agenda, which allows it to legitimise itself through accumulation, conversion, and transformation of social, economic, and symbolic capitals into political capital and vice versa. When Hizbullah earns political capital, the Party spends it by investing it into more and more cultural and socio-economic capitals in line with its civilisational mission of accomplishing social justice in line with the tenets of Shi'ite jurisprudence. This is one way of demonstrating how Hizbullah employs its capitals as forms of resource mobilisation, as its 'progressive' identity allows it a large margin of manoeuvre.

As a resisting public, the Taliban displayed their social protest as a manifestation of resistance identity. Building on a long historical precedent and an established disciplined tradition of resisting, fighting, and struggling against aggression and foreign invasion, the Taliban were able to uphold their resistance identity through a holy matrimony between their nationalistic tribal traditions, on the one hand, and their religious beliefs and sensibilities, on the other. They were successful in confronting aggression because their collective identity and shared consciousness/memory are based upon the dictum that occupation will end one day through their active resistance, through their cherished resistance identity. However, their success in the cultural sphere was limited and short lived, being the result of repression and power politics. They were firm and adamant in not making concessions on their doctrinal views that severely ground music and negatively affect cultural production. Largely, they were consistent in their behaviour of applying 'severe' punishments (*hudud*) to breaches of their edits, based on their doctrinal interpretation of Islamic law. However, this experience was short-lived in Afghan history since it ran contrary to established traditions that are against stifling freedoms, music, and dance, which form the backbone of the Pashtu folklore and cultural heritage. This explains why, when the Taliban's repression ended and their regime lost power in 2001, people returned to their long-standing traditions of incorporating and celebrating music and dance in cultural productions. Thus, the people opted for reconciliation, rather than conflict, even the ethnic Pashtu—who historically cherish and practice the *Attan* dance that is accompanied by musicians playing *Dhols* (frame drums), *Tablaas* (percussions), and wooden flutes—opted for such an option (Sarafraz 2008: 139ff, 330-336; Rashid 2008: ; Baily 2009: 160-162). Baily concludes, "Not only do we see (yet again) how sensitive an indicator of broad social and cultural processes music is, but how fiercely control over music is contested. One ponders the mystery of what it is about music that makes it so powerful, and how that power might be harnessed for performances of reconciliation instead of conflict" (2009: 163).

Thus, as a resisting public, the Taliban were more successful in facing foreign invasion and occupation, than in stifling freedom of thought, speech, and cultural expression. This might explain why these practices backfired on them and prevented them from moving to a project identity that ought to be based upon conviction, rather than coercion or necessity, as Castells admonished. Since the Taliban's project was local and specific, from the stance of their 'narrow' particularity, they did not have much interest in sampling and construing the workings of globalisation, without which 'dominant interests enacted by global flows of capital, power, and information' cannot be achieved, again as Castells convincingly argued.

Conversely, as a resisting public, Hizbullah was able to shift from the restrictive politics of a narrow exclusive identity to the more encompassing project identity based upon the mobilisation of its intellectual and cultural resources. The Party accomplished this through the 'collective language' of art; by way of harnessing the power of music, and the music in power; and through the resilience of its religious culture and identity. This new jurisprudence leads to dramatic transformations that translate themselves into an Islamic project identity grounded in dominant interests. As an extension of Hizbullah's project identity based on communal resistance, the Islamic project identity relies upon an interdependent-conducive relationship between the leaders and religious scholars (*'ulama*), the kinetic energy of social transformation, on the one hand, and the populace, the catalysts of that transformation, on the other. Thus, Hizbullah seems on the way of achieving 'dominant interests enacted by global flows of capital, power, and information'.

And so, for Hizbullah 'jihad with music' and 'resistance art', not only serve as a medium for the negotiation of power, but also become a space for resisting, weakening, and challenging the hegemonic ideology and authority of the state by enforcing Hizbullah as a 'resisting public'. From this stance, music accumulates symbolic capital by way of resource mobilisation. Thus, music becomes a subtle vehicle for agency and empowerment in the service of enforcing cultural politics and cultural citizenship. It seems Baily's hypothesis proved to be true—'the chronic absence of music is symptomatic of a dysfunctional society' (Baily 2009: 160) —as was the case with the Taliban when they were in power; and

'Islamic cultures, which are tolerant towards music are likely to be liberal in other respects, and music is a sensitive indicator of a whole set of other values and attitudes' (Baily 2009: 145) —as seems to be the case with Hizbullah.

References

Fadi 'Abbas, *Zaman Al-Intasarat [Days of Victory]*, (Beirut: Dar Al-Hadi, 2009).

Joseph Alagha, *Hizbullah's Identity Construction*, (Amsterdam: Amsterdam University Press, 2011).

Joseph Alagha, 'Pious Entertainment: Hizbullah's Islamic Cultural Sphere', in *Muslim Rap, Halal Soaps and Revolutionary Theater: Artistic Developments in the Muslim World*. Karin van Nieuwkerk (ed.), (Austin: University of Texas Press, 2011), pp. 149-175.

Joseph Alagha, 'A Tug of War: Hizbullah, Participation, and Contestation in the Lebanese Public Sphere', in *Publics, Politics and Participation: Locating the Public Sphere in the Middle East and North Africa*. Seteney Shami (ed.), (New York: Social Science Research Council of America, 2009), pp. 457-487.

Joseph Alagha, *The Shifts in Hizbullah's Ideology*, (Amsterdam: Amsterdam University Press, 2006).

A. Yusuf Ali, *The Holy Qur'an: Translation and Commentary*, Fourth printing, (Lahore: Islamic Propagation Centre, 1993).

Muhammad 'Amara, *Al-Ghina' wa Al-Musiqa: Halal am Haram? [Singing and Music: Religiously Sanctioned or Prohibited?]*, Series of Islamic Enlightenment, 33, (Cairo: Dar Nahdat Misr Ltd., 1999).

Anon, *Majalis Al-Afrah [Celebration of Feasts]*, (Beirut: Cultural Islamic Al-Ma'arif Association, 2007).

Khalid Baig, *Slippery Stone: an inquiry into Islam's stance on music*, Garden Grove, (CA: Openmind Press 2008).

John Baily, 'Music and Censorship in Afghanistan, 1973-2003', in *Music and the Play of Power: Music, Politics, and Ideology in the Middle East, North Africa, and Central Asia*. Laudan Nooshin (ed.), SOAS Musicology Series: Ashgate, 2009, pp. 143-163.

John Baily, *'Can you Stop the Birds Singing?' The Censorship of Music in Afghanistan*, ISSN 1601-2127, Freemuse, (Copenhagen: Handy-Print).

Pierre Bourdieu, 'The Field of Cultural Production', in *the Polity Reader in Cultural Theory*, (Cambridge: Cambridge University Press, 1994), pp. 50-65.

Pierre Bourdieu, *The Field of Cultural Production*, (Cambridge: Polity Press, 1993).

Pierre Bourdieu, *In Other Words: Essays Towards a Reflexive Sociology*, (Cambridge: Polity Press, 1990).

Pierre Bourdieu, 'Genèse et structure du champ religieux', *Revue française de sociologie*, 12: 295-334, 1971.

Craig Calhoun(ed), *Social Theory and the Politics of Identity*, (Oxford: Blackwell Publishers, 1994).

Manuel Castells, *The Rise of the Network Society. (The Information Age: Economy, Society, and Culture, Volume I)*. Second edition, (Oxford: Blackwell Publishers Ltd., 2000).

Manuel Castells, *The Power of Identity, (The Information Age: Economy, Society, and Culture, Volume II)*. Second edition. (Oxford: Blackwell Publishers Ltd., 1998, 2004).

Neera Chandhoke, *State and Civil Society: Explorations in Political Theory*, (London: Sage Publications, 1995).

Nadia Crete, *Al-Ibda' fi Al-Musiqa: Bayna Al-Irda' wa Al-Alam [Creativity in Music: Between Satisfaction and Pain]*, (Beirut: Bissan, 2008).

Freemuse, *Music Will Not Be Silenced: Third Freemuse World Conference On Music & Censorship, Istanbul*, November 25-26, 2006.

Freemuse, *First World Conference on Music and Censorship, Copenhagen, November 20-22 1998*, ISBN 87-988163-0-6. Denmark, 2001.

Graham E. Fuller, *The Future of Political Islam*, (New York: Palgrave, Macmillan, 2003).

Joshua S. Goldstein, *International Relations*, Fifth Edition, (New York: Longman, 2003).

Antonio Gramsci, *Selections from the Prison Notebooks of Antonio Gramsci* (trans. and ed. Quinton Hoare and Geoffrey Nowell Smith), (London: Lawrence and Wishart, 1971).

Jurgen Habermas, *Theory of Communicative Action*, (Cambridge: Polity Press, 1987).

Sayyid Hashim Hamidi, *Al-Ghina' wa Alat Al-Tarab [Singing and the Instruments of Enchantment]*,(Tehran: Markaz Nashr Jami'at Al-'Ilm wa Al-Sun'a fi Iran, 1994).

Muhammad Abd Al-Husayn Hammud, *Al-Qawl al-Fasl bi Hurmat al-Ghina' fi al-'Urs [The Final Word on Prohibiting Singing in Weddings]*, (Beirut: Dar al-Manhal al-Lubnani, 2005).

Abd Al-Rahman Al-Jaziri, *Al-Fiqh 'ala Al-Madhahib Al-Arba'a [Jurisprudence Based on the Four Sunni Schools of Law]*, (Cairo: Mu'assat Al-Mukhtar, 2001).

Ousmane Kane, *Muslim Modernity in Postcolonial Nigeria: A Study of the Society for the Removal of Innovation and Reinstatement of Tradition*, (Leiden: Brill, 2003).

Marie Korpe(ed.), *Shoot the Singer! Music Censorship Today*, (London: Zed Books, 2004).

Imam 'Ali Khamina'i, *Al-Fann Al-Islami 'inda Al-Imam Al-Qa'id [Islamic Art According to Imam Khamina'i]*, Compiled by Muhammad Salar, the Cultural Attaché of the Islamic Republic in Lebanon, (Beirut: Dar Al-Mahajja al-Bayda', 2009).

Imam 'Ali Khamina'i, *Al-Kalimat Al-Qisar [Aphorisms]*, (Beirut: Cultural Islamic Al-Ma'arif Association, 2006).

Imam 'Ali Khamina'i, *Ajwibat Al-Istifta'at [Answers to Questions]*, Second Part, (Iraq: Karbala', 2004).

Abu Al-Qasim Khu'i, *Minhaj Al-Salihin [The Curriculum of the Righteous]*, (Qumm: Madinat Al-'Ilm, 1990).

Krister Malm (ed.), *Human Rights for Musicians*, ISBN 978-87-988163-2-4, Freemuse, (Copenhagen: Handy-Print, 2008).

Muhammad Jawad Mughniyyé, *'Ilm Usual Al-Fiqh fi Thawbihi Al-Jadid [The Science of the Principles of Jurisprudence in its New Garment]*, (Beirut: Dar Al-Tayyar Al-Jadid, 1988).

Laudan Nooshin (ed.), *Music and the Play of Power: Music, Politics and Ideology in the Middle East, North Africa and Central Asia*, SOAS Musicology Series: Ashgate, 2009.

Muhammad Husayn Sbayti, , '*Jidariyyat Al-Nasr*: For a Resistance that Produced Art, and for an Art that Contributed to Portraying the Victory', *Al-Intiqadnet*: http://www.moqawama.org/essaydetailsf.php?eid=16447&fid=48. Accessed on February 15, 2010.

Muhammad Sarafraz, *Harakat Al-Taliban min Al-Nushu' Ila al-Suqut [The Taliban: From the Founding to the Collapse]*, (Beirut: Dar Al-Mizan, 2008).

Georg Sørensen and Robert Jackson, *Introduction to International Relations: Theories and approaches*, Second Edition, (Oxford: Oxford University Press, 2003).

John Thompson, 'Social Theory, Mass Communication and Public Life', in *The Polity Reader in Cultural Theory*, (Cambridge: Cambridge University Press, 1994), pp. 24-37.

Karin Van Nieuwkerk (ed.), *Muslim Rap, Halal Soaps and Revolutionary Theater. Artistic Developments in the Muslim World*, (Austin: University of Texas Press, 2011).

Karin van Nieuwkerk (ed.), 'Of Morals, Missions and the Market New Religiosity and "Art with a Mission" in Egypt', in *Muslim Rap, Halal Soaps and Revolutionary Theater: Artistic Developments in the Muslim World*, (Austin: University of Texas Press, 2011), pp. 177-204.

Dr. Yusuf Abdallah Al-Qaradawi, *Fiqh Al-Ghina' wa Al-Musiqa fi Daw' Al-Qur'an wa Al-Sunna [The Jurisprudence of Singing and Music in Light of the Qur'an and Traditions]*, Third edition, (Cairo: Maktabat Wehbé, 2004).

Tariq Ramadan, *Radical Reform. Islamic Ethics and Liberation*, (Oxford: Oxford University Press, 2009).

Ahmad Rashid, *Taliban, Islam, Oil and the New Great Game in Central Asia*. Second revised edition, (London: I. B. Taurus, 2008).

Muhammad Sarafraz, *Harakat Al-Taliban min Al-Nushu' Ila al-Suqut [The Taliban: From the Founding to the Collapse]*, (Beirut: Dar Al-Mizan, 2008).

Hans Wehr, *A Dictionary of Modern Written Arabic*, (Beirut: Librairie du Liban, 1980).

Jessica Winegar, 'Purposeful Art between Television Preachers and the State', (Autumn 2008), *ISIM Review* 22: 28-29.

Notes

1. Khalid Baig, *Slippery Stone: an inquiry into Islam's stance on music*, First edition, Garden Grove, (CA: Openmind Press, 2008), 'Preface' and pp. 4-5.
2. Ibid. p. 277.
3. Ibid. p. XIII.
4. For instance, see http://vocfm.co.za/blogs/munadia/?p=223, accessed on April 29, 2010.
5. Ibid. p. XIII.
6. Ibid. pp. XIV-XV.
7. Ibid. p. XIX.
8. Ibid. p. XVIII.
9. Ibid. pp. 4-5.
10. Ibid. pp. 70-74.
11. Ibid. p. 77.
12. Ibid. p. 95.
13. Ibid. p. 91.
14. Ibid. p. 83.
15. Ibid. p. 127.
16. Ibid. p. 10:
17. Ibid. pp. 167-174.
18. Ibid. p. 169.
19. Ibid. p. 203.
20. Ibid. p. 192.
21. Ibid. p. 3.
22. Ibid. p. 275.
23. Ibid. p. 3.
24. Ibid. p. 77.
25. Ibid. p. 277.
26. Baig discredits al-Qaradawi because he used to listen to Umm Kalthum, whose 'voice numbs the people instead of arousing them'. He criticises al-Qaradawi because for him 'music was a matter of personal choice. It was fine if you listened to it and fine if you did not' (Baig 2008: 66).
27. Enchantment "Refers to emotions related to extreme joy or extreme sorrow and also employs sensual pleasure" and "Sensual pleasure caused by listening to music" (Baig 2008: 6, 335).
28. See http://www.sistani.org/local.php?modules=nav&nid=2&bid=53&pid=2808&hl=music: Music, singing & dancing » General Rules, accessed on July 17, 2009.
29. See Qur'an (25:72). According to al-Tabari, *laghu* is 'all speech and actions that are baseless or abhorrent... *laghu* is neither beneficial nor harmful and therefore it remains permissible' (Baig 2008: 116).
30. Thus, al-Albani is even more stringent than al-Tabari in his dealing with *laghu*. *Al-Sala Magazine*, vol. 2 (15 *Jamada al-Aghira* 1413/ December 15, 1992), as cited in

www.saaid.net/fatwa/f46.htm, a Salafi website that Baig referred to more than once, accessed on May 05, 2009.

31. http://www.youtube.com/watch?v=CrBB_yHLJiU&feature=related, accessed on February 06, 2010.
32. *Al-Jihad al-asghar*, or smaller (military) *jihad*, signifies struggle (holy war) against the enemies of Islam. This defensive jihad ought to be distinguished from *al-Jihad al-akbar*, or greater jihad, which is struggle against the self and its desires (*jihad al-nafs*), or the affirmation of the individual's service for the cause of religion.
33. Although this article has been thoroughly researched, I neither claim expertise on the Taliban nor the Pashtu.
34. Resistance identities incorporate an array of various movements, which dwell upon religious fundamentalism, nationalism, socialism, ethnic identity, and territorial identity (urban movements and local communities). (Sørensen and Jackson 2003: 219).
35. The Soviets, from 1979-89; and the US and its NATO allies from 2001 to the present.
36. 'Greetings to you Mudabar Jana' means greetings to our dear; one who is dear like life. The word '*jaan*' in Farsi, Urdu, and Pashtu means 'life'. People say 'my *jaan*' to address one who is very close; one who is loved so much, very dear.
37. www.welaya-hlb.com, accessed on July 17, 2009.
38. The header of Hizbullah's now defunct website www.hizbollah.org referred to the following Qur'anic verse: "We wish to favour the downtrodden [oppressed] in the land and make them leaders [Imams] and make them the inheritors; And establish (*numakin*) them firmly in the land..." (28:5-6). Other Qur'anic verses signifying *tamkin* are quoted by Hizbullah: (12:21); (12:56); (12:54); (18:84); (7:10); (46:26); (6:6); (22:41); (18:95); and (28:57).

39 .welaya-hlb.com, accessed on July 17, 2009.

40. *Zajal*: 'popular Arabic poem in strophic form' (using the same music for successive stanzas) (Hans Wehr 1980: 374).
41. http://www.youtube.com/watch?v=DM1hU9zIPlg&feature=related, accessed on July 17, 2009.
42. 'Hezbollah also sees itself committed in introducing the true picture of Islam, the Islam that is logical. Committed to introduce the civilized Islam to humanity'. Hizbullah's 2004 self-description: 'Identity and goals'.
43. '*Ghazy*' is a Pashto nashid with English subtitles, but with no musical instruments. Contains a slideshow of the mujahidin in Paktia: http://www.youtube.com/watch?v=JfqiKY41RBo (3.42), accessed July 17, 2009.
44. This also calls for an explanation. Life is like a rose, and the *mujahid*/*Ghazy* wants to 'harm' (poison) this life for the sake of Allah. I reckon the metaphor of poison has been used to describe 'harm', and poison also leads to death. No one would harm or destroy a beautiful rose, but a *mujahid*/*Ghazy* harms or sacrifices (poisons) the flower (life) for the sake of Allah or in the way of God (*fi sabili Allah*).
45. Ends with a fading sound, a practice similar to professional musicians.

46. For the anthem in full, see http://www.youtube.com/watch?v=idLyEv20ETM&feature=related, accessed on July 17, 2009.

47 The Qur'anic verse (33:33) has been interpreted to signify the sinlessness of the Prophet, his daughter Fatima and the twelve Imams. This has also been demonstrated by Shi'ite traditions, the most salient being: "I [Prophet Muhammad], 'Ali, Hasan, Husayn and nine of the descendants of Husayn are pure and sinless" (Alagha 2006: 72).

48. Afghan Pashto nashid with English subtitles, but with echo effects. Accessed on July 17, 2009: http://www.youtube.com/watch?v=-tp7LvKIIA4 (43.41).

49. It lies in ruin.

50. After being bombed.

51. Ya Aba 'Abdi Allah nahnu ummat Hizbullah [Oh Imam Husayn we are the nation of Hizbullah] (Iraqi accent of *marathi*: wailing rituals) http://www.youtube.com/watch?v=F1jlNGnONdl, accessed on July 17, 2009.

52. Direct descendents of the Prophet.

53. Categories of punishment range from flogging for petty breaches, to beheading as a chastisement for killing, to cutting the hand as a castigation for theft.

54. "I was assured that this drum had not been banned, because, according to tradition, Prophet Mohammad is said to have sanctioned its use on a festive occasion" (Malm 2008: 61). (i.e. the Prophet sanctioned this form of pious entertainment).

55. Khalid Baig, *Slippery Stone: an Inquiry into Islam's Stance on Music.* First edition. Garden Grove, (CA: Openmind Press, 2008), p. 262.

56. Ibid. p. 77.

57. Ibid. p. 93.

58. Ibid. pp. 105ff. "To prevent keeping pigeons and playing with birds. Within ten day this habit/hobby should stop. After ten days this should be monitored and the pigeons and any other playing birds should be killed" (Rashid 2008: 218-219).

59. n. 55, pp. 68-69.

60. Ibid. p. 91.

61. Ibid. p. 69.

62. Ibid. p. 271.

63. Ibid. p. 262.

64. Ibid. p. 267.

65. Ibid. See for instance, pp. xvii-xviii, 8, 52, 70, 72, 75, 255, 258, 268-9, 277, etc.

66. Ibid. p. 264.

67. Ibid. p. 263.

68. Ibid. p. 265.

69. Ibid. pp. 218, 264.

70. Cf. "Art is an obligation for Muslims… We will not be able to carry out *Nahda* [Renaissance] without Art…art as a tool of progress" (Winegar 2008: 28-29).

71. www.welaya-hlb.com, accessed on July 17, 2009.

72. www.welaya-hlb.com, accessed on July 17, 2009.

73. Personal Interview, August 11, 2009. Al-Musawi worked at al-Manar TV as political program's editor and was the editor-in-chief of Hizbullah's weekly mouthpiece *al-*

Intiqad. He holds a Ph.D. in Islamic studies from Birmingham University.

74. Personal interview, October 21, 2009.
75. Personal interview, October 16, 2009.
76. Fayyad was referring to the Qur'anic verse (7:33): "The things that my Lord has indeed forbidden are: shameful deeds/debaucheries, whether open or secret". Baig shares the same view with Fayyad (2008: 218, 264).
77. Personal interview, October 06, 2009.
78. Personal interview, August 04, 2009.
79. Personal interview, October 06, 2009.
80. Personal interview, August 10, 2009.
81. Baig defines *tarab* as 'sensuous music for fun and entertainment' (2008: 8, 52).
82. Personal interview, October 06, 2009.
83. Personal interview, October 16, 2009.
84. Personal interview, October 16, 2009.
85. Reiterated in personal interviews with Shaykh 'Ali Daher and Muhammad Kawtharini, respectively the president and the vice-president of Hizbullah's Cultural Unit, August 07 and October 22, 2009.
86. Personal interview with Shaykh Akram Barakat, October 16, 2009.
87. According to Bourdieu, cultural capital refers mainly to education, culture, and related skills. Cultural resilience is a currency of social capital and networking (1971: 295-334).
88. Personal interview, October 19, 2009.
89. See Qasim's introduction to ('Abbas 2009: 6-7). The book contains a host of mobilisation poems, including the most played song after the July 2006 war: '*Nasrak Hazz al-Dini* (Your Victory Shook the World)': http://www.welaya-hlb.com/palysong.php?id=84; http://www.welaya-hlb.com/sub.php?op=new#. Accessed on September 26, 2009. This book has been published to commemorate 'Beirut as an International Book Capital'. Poet Fadi 'Abbas is the minutes taker (*amin al-sirr*) of *Al-Ma'arif Al-Hikmiyya* College.
90. Personal interview, October 21, 2009.
91. Personal interview, October 22, 2009.
92. www.welaya-hlb.com, accessed on July 17, 2009.
93. http://www.youtube.com/watch?v=idLyEv20ETM&feature=related, accessed on July 17, 2009.
94. http://www.welaya-hlb.com/sub.php?op=new#, accessed on July 17, 2009.
95. See DVD entitled 'Whisper' produced by 'The Lebanese Association of Arts', and www.orchestra-hlb.com; http://www.orchestra-hlb.com/materials/works.htm, accessed on July 17, 2009.
96. In 2005, it was licensed by the Lebanese government and it was registered in the Ministry of Interior under number 295 AD, as published in the Official Gazette. As Muhammad Kawtharani told me, *Risalat* is actively engaged in implementing it three-year strategic plan (2009-2012) in order to keep on promoting 'committed Islamic culture' through resistance art. Personal interview, August 07, 2009.